Why Poetry Sucks

An Anthology of Humorous Experimental Canadian
Poetry in English Written by Canadians for Canadians
(or American Bodysnatchers) in the Early Years of the
21st Century with an Overly Long and
Not That Clever Subtitle the Publisher Rightly Refused
to Put on the Cover

Edited by Ryan Fitzpatrick & Jonathan Ball

INSOMNIAC PRESS

Library and Archives Canada Cataloguing in Publication

Why poetry sucks / Jonathan Ball and Ryan Fitzpatrick.

Issued in print and electronic formats.
ISBN 978-1-55483-122-7 (pbk.).--ISBN 978-1-55483-141-8 (html)

1. Experimental poetry, Canadian (English). 2. Canadian poetry (English)--20th century. 3. Canadian poetry (English)-- 21st century. I. Ball, Jonathan, 1979-, editor II. Fitzpatrick, Ryan, 1978-, editor

PS8293.W49 2014   C811'.5408011   C2014-903293-5
                                                 C2014-903294-3

The publisher gratefully acknowledges the support of the Canada Council, the Ontario Arts Council, and the Department of Canadian Heritage through the Canada Book Fund.

Printed and bound in Canada

Insomniac Press
520 Princess Avenue, London, Ontario, Canada, N6B 2B8
www.insomniacpress.com

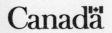

RECLINER OF CONTENTS

"TAKE THESE POEMS — PLEASE!": AN INTRODUCTION

Ryan Fitzpatrick & Jonathan Ball

"I had to let in the comedy, and not just for laughs' sake, but because it undoes things."
— Robert Kroetsch[1]

"Why does poetry suck?" This question echoes down the ages and is echoed by undergraduate students, eyes glazing as they gaze upon their reading lists. "It doesn't," we tell them, but in our hearts, we know different. We know it does.[2]

What sucks about poetry? The short answer is the words, and their combinations. The longer answer has to do with how so few of those combinations include the pairing "Nacho Tuesdays." Yes, poetry seems to lack nachos, and, aside from that, it seems to lack humour. Indeed, no literary genre appears less funny than poetry, where conventional wisdom has it that a "good poem" must move the reader to some epiphany through the subtle revelation of some aspect of the human condition, the least funny condition of all.[3]

If poetry's condition seems serious, then is experimen-

---

[1] Shirley Neuman and Robert Wilson, *Labyrinths of Voice: Conversations with Robert Kroetsch* (Edmonton: NeWest, 1982), 178.
[2] Yes, we know footnotes suck too. Give us a break!
[3] Even leprosy has its lighter moments. Look, Ma, no hands!

tal poetry in critical condition? Carmine Starnino, constant critic, has declared that "humourlessness" is "the most galling failure of our current crop of experimental phenoms" in an essay otherwise surprisingly generous to experimental phenom bpNichol.[4] Complaints like Starnino's are common and, in many ways, true. While poetry as a cultural activity is funny,[5] and the idea that we should take poetry seriously is funny, actually taking poetry seriously isn't very funny at all — and neither are most poems.

At the risk of not being funny,[6] we should complain that Starnino is correct only in a technical sense. Humourlessness *is* the most galling failure of experimental poets, because it is the most galling failure of poets and poetry overall. We balk at Starnino's implicit suggestion, which is that experimental poetry is, in a general sense, *more humourless* than conventional poetry. In fact, when conventional poetry is funny, it is often funny because it has incorporated lessons from experimental poetry (usually, earlier avant-gardes). Often, these avant-garde movements and authors take themselves seriously, or too seriously, but then lighten up and begin to fall into self-parody as their assumptions and techniques are incorporated (or mocked) by the mainstream — Surrealism is the most obvious example. More recently, we have seen the opposite trajectory with the American post-avant[7] Flarf writers, who began

---

[4] Carmine Starnino, "bpNichol," *Lazy Bastardism: Essays & Reviews on Contemporary Poetry* (Kentville, NS: Gaspereau, 2012), 165.

[5] Really, what's more hilarious than all those loser poets taking themselves so seriously, sweating about whether or not they should employ an Oxford comma?

[6] We're already well under the sitcom standard of three jokes per page.

by parodying bad conventional poetry but ended up taking the joke more seriously and more politically as bad conventional poetry became a primary way to address the national trauma of 9/11.[8]

In other words, galling humourlessness is not a defining trait of experimental poetry — the work is often intentionally funny, because it uses humour in particular ways, or unintentionally funny, due to its relative strangeness or how removed it seems from something we should take seriously. As a result of its emphasis on attentive and playful work with the material of language, experimental poetry may even have a different, perhaps closer, relationship to humour than so-called "conventional" poetry. But why? Where's the beef?

When people criticize experimental poetry, in essays or reviews or bars, they often criticize the work on one of two fronts (aesthetically speaking): either (1) it's dry and boring, inelegantly flaunting its theoretical foundations to become robotic and joyless — in sum, *it takes itself too seriously*; or, (2) it's gibberish, fraudulent, pointless — the writer is just playing around, being silly, and the whole thing is just *not serious enough*. Either humourless or "just jokes," experimental poetry can't win. Submerged here is the notion that writing *can* include humour (if it has to)

---

[7] More on this term below.

[8] Not to mention the fact that cloyingly idiotic poetry gained a political timbre in the face of one of the most celebrated idiots in presidential history.

but *not too much* or it ceases to be "literary." Either there's nothing human in it (no humour, no emotions, just theory-speak) or it's all too human, an idiot pleasure, one not worthy of being called "poetry."

If poetry can't be funny when it's poetry and can't be poetry when it's funny, what can be done to rehabilitate comedy's public image in the literary world, not to mention in experimental poetry? If comedy can't win an Oscar, how will it ever win the Griffin?[9] Throughout literary history, comedy has had its defenders, but something always seemed to go awry. Aristotle dropped the ball by not backing up the second volume of his *Poetics* (the one about comedy) in the cloud or on a flash drive. Freud started to make a useful connection between humour and language in *Jokes and Their Relation to the Unconscious* but then became more interested in cocaine.[10]

Help comes from an unlikely hero: Russian Formalist Victor Shklovsky. Shklovsky theorized that art makes use of a fundamental technique he called *defamiliarization*:

> The purpose of art is to impart the sensation of things as they are perceived and not as they are known. The technique of art is to make objects "unfamiliar," to make forms difficult, to increase the difficulty and length of perception because the

---

[9] And how could it accept the award with a straight face? (Acknowledging that, yes, some of the folks in this book have accepted awards with straight faces. Isn't that funny?)

[10] Jonathan insisted that we cut Ryan's joke about Freud's sexual hang-ups on the grounds that it was too hacky. Is it Ryan's fault Freud liked to have sex with wolves? [The answer might surprise you: Yes!]

process of perception is an aesthetic end in itself
and must be prolonged.[11]

Both the joke and poetry operate in this way, by making
our language and our social operations *strange*. Thus, de-
familiarization is, arguably, the basic gesture of poetry —
poetry takes language and pushes it past the limits of its
quotidian use, to estrange us from language and its trans-
parent, communicative capacity (i.e., how we typically en-
counter language in our everyday lives) — poetic
techniques, from the use of rhyme to line breaks and so
on, typically have this purpose of manipulating the lan-
guage to estrange it so that it *means more*. The effect of
this estrangement could be to heighten its power of ex-
pression (as in most lyrical poetry), engage with its mate-
riality (as in much experimental poetry), or to attach its
signifiers to inappropriate but (il)logically justifiable sig
nifieds (as in jokes predicated on wordplay). Similarly,
jokes not predicated on wordplay generally work in the
way that (according to Shklovsky) Leo Tolstoy works: by
describing our social or political activities, or unexamined
assumptions and ideologies, so that what only a minute
before the joke seemed natural and normal now seems
nonsensical and bizarre.[12]

  This tension or gap between the familiar and the poet's

---

[11] Victor Shklovsky, "Art as Technique" (1917), *The Critical
Tradition: Classic Texts and Contemporary Trends*, ed. David H.
Richter (Boston: Bedford, 1989), 741.
[12] Shklovsky notes that "Tolstoy described the dogmas and rituals he
attacked as if they were unfamiliar, substituting everyday meanings
for the customarily religious meanings of the words common in

or comedian's attempts to estrange us from it often works like the experimentalist technique of the Situationist *détournement* (altering the already existing in a small way, to reveal or otherwise subvert its hidden operations) or by producing a gap between our expectations and their demolition. Let's get super unfunny for few minutes.[13] Working from the Lacanian idea of the *point de capiton* or quilting point, the idea that meaning is retroactively determined by the final word in a statement, Alenka Zupančič frames the punchline in terms of this Lacanian operation.[14] As the sentence moves forward ("Dick and Jane were exposed to …"), the meaning of the whole statement changes depending on how it ends ("harmful radiation," "foreign languages," "their uncle the exhibitionist").[15] For Zupančič, humour can serially chain in this way, altering the terms of discourse to comic effect through continual additions (like when comedians add "tags" after punchlines) — the sentence never really ends; it just keeps mutating. The joke becomes an elaborate game of misdirection, setting up the audience for one outcome and then delivering another, producing a surprising

church ritual. Many persons were painfully wounded; they considered it blasphemy to present as strange and monstrous what they accepted as sacred" (Shklovsky, "Art as Technique," 744). It's not hard to imagine comedian David Cross doing the same thing, for the same reason, and getting the same reaction.

[13] Slap yourself in the face a few times to sober up your thoughts.

[14] Alenka Zupančič, *The Odd One In: On Comedy* (Cambridge: MIT, 2008).

[15] This example is paraphrased from Bruce Fink, *Lacan to the Letter: Reading Écrits Closely* (Minneapolis: U of Minnesota P, 2004), 89-90.

surplus for the reader — an answer to a question that was never asked.

The classic example of this misdirection in comedy (one now so conventional that it's easy to overlook the actual subversive logic of how this joke operates) is comedian Henny Youngman's "Take my wife — please!" Youngman sets us up to believe that he is about to use his wife as an example of the sort of foolishness he's just been discussing ("Now, take my wife for instance …"), but he's trying to pawn her off on us instead, suggesting rather than stating the reasons why. The key to this is his timing, turning the anticipated outcome of a textual or situational thread into something else entirely. Comic timing, then, becomes the act of delivering the blow when the audience is most vulnerable, tipping the world over into disorder at the audience's point of highest comfort. The punchline trades in a kind of affective disorientation, a powerful example of language creating effects on the body. Playing out as a gentle trauma, comedy both scrambles our discourse *and* provokes a physical reaction. If we are unable to speak in the face of it, it's because we're rolling in the aisles.

Both comedy and poetry can exploit this "quilting" ability of the punchline to work in resistance to dominant social codes. Both practices are able to produce short circuits that lay bare hidden ideological operations. These hidden operations are composed of material processes and assemblages that, for one reason or another, we are unable to see — the classic comedic example being Karl Marx's observation of the hidden labour embedded in commodities.[16] The production of this gap, and of a short circuit that seems to close but really exposes it, is key to most satire, from Jonathan Swift's "A Modest Proposal" to Sacha Baron Cohen's mockumentary film *Borat*, as well as politically minded experimental poetry. In other words, comedy and satire expose how something appears to make logical sense even when it doesn't, exposing a gap in understanding as it tries to hide it, like someone scrambling to get an elephant out through the bedroom window so their partner doesn't see it.

Consider, for example, "The Last Temptation of Krust," a 1998 episode of *The Simpsons* that slyly comments on the role of comedy as political critique.[17] When Krusty the Clown performs at a stand-up comedy benefit against soil erosion, he launches into a routine of hack jokes about, primarily, TV dinners. Antiquated and unfunny, his jokes bomb. In response, Krusty turns to an ugly display of yellowface dripping with every stereotype imaginable (buck teeth, deep bowing, *r*'s replaced with *l*'s). The crowd is stunned at his old-fashioned racism and begins to boo, so Krusty pulls out his "A-material": a flapping dickey. After failed attempts to reform his act, Krusty decides to retire from comedy.

Until he doesn't. After a press conference where reporters explode with laughter at his raw, snarky dissatisfaction with contemporary comedy (he complains

---

[16] What a riot!

[17] "The Last Temptation of Krust," *The Simpsons: The Complete Ninth Season*, DVD (1998; Los Angeles: Twentieth Century Fox Home Entertainment LLC, 2006).

that people no longer want to listen to "time-tested jokes about women drivers and doctor's bills"), Krusty announces his triumphant return. He proceeds to "tell it like it is" — in other words, to speak truth to power. He delivers blow after blow to the very consumerism once integral to his personality. "So, I'm watching TV today, and all I keep seeing is dead celebrities hawking products. They got poor Vincent Price floating around on a toilet cake telling me about the horrors of an unfresh bowl!" The on-screen audience is moved to a shared moment of anger, lighting cash on fire at Krusty's suggestion. For the off-screen audience, the humour in Krusty's joke comes from the contrast between his two stage personas. In "retirement," Krusty becomes an inverted version of poor Vincent Price, killing his product-hawking prior self to re-emerge as a critically minded political comedian. Order soon returns to the program, and Krusty returns to his unfunny product-shilling self. For a brief moment, however, Krusty seems like he might present a minor threat to capitalist undertakings, forwarding a counter-consumerist discourse that has social effects.[18]

Key to the second Krusty's more critical approach to humour is a sense of the joke as a kind of attack — an understanding central to both radical and reactionary senses of humour. In other words, the rearticulations humour is

---

[18] Underlying all of this, of course, is a critique of anti-consumerist experimental comedy as unfunny and hypocritical at its core, "selling" the idea of not-buying. In fact, it is *because* Krusty pushes the crowd to burn money with his anti-consumer tirade that some executives approach him to be the spokesperson for an unsafe station wagon.

capable of can be used to *violently* upend situations and understandings. In his discussion of "tendentious" jokes, Freud sets up an encounter where the joke becomes a means of exclusion.[19] Let's set up Freud's serious social analysis as a kind of joke to underline how funny it's not. A man walks into a bar. Across the room, he sees a woman and is immediately smitten. He approaches her, and they strike up a conversation. A second man walks up to the same woman. She finds herself more attracted to him, turning away from the first man. Angry, the first man insults the woman, and the second man laughs.[20] Rather than being read as the attack it is, a joke is born out of this homosocial interaction, where the two men connect over their mutual exclusion of the woman. For Freud, "[t]he smut becomes a joke and is only tolerated when it has the character of a joke" (100).[21] This structure of attack and exclusion isn't limited to attacks against women, but it is an effect of power and privilege, meaning the attack can

---

[19] In Chapter 3 of Sigmund Freud, *Jokes and Their Relation to the Unconscious* (London: Hogarth, 1960), ed. and trans. James Strachey.
[20] Freud's narration is far more serious and analytical than this. His work points to seduction, its failures, and its homosocial successes: "When the first person finds his libidinal impulse inhibited by the woman, he develops a hostile trend against that second person and calls on the originally interfering third person as his ally. Through the first person's smutty speech, the woman is exposed before the third, who, as listener, has now been bribed by the effortless satisfaction of his own libido" (100).
[21] This is a strength of humour as well, allowing us to confront the traumatic through the relatively safe lens of the joke. Unless we're talking about 9/11 — then we need the inspiring seriousness of poetry. Or Gilbert Gottfried.

also be directed at race, ethnicity, sexual orientation, disability, etc. Remember that what sends Krusty into his critical tirades is his anger over the fact that he can no longer be successful as the white patriarchal clown, since jokes about flapping dickies and women drivers (and other "classics") get shouted down in disgust.

Let's turn now to a June 2012 stand-up set by Daniel Tosh at the Laugh Factory in Hollywood.[22] A woman in the audience calls Tosh out ("heckles" him) during a part of his act where he asserts that anything, including rape, can be funny. In the woman's account,[23] she yells out, "Actually, rape jokes are never funny!" and Tosh, in response, poses a hypothetical question/threat: "Wouldn't it be funny if that girl got raped by, like, five guys right now? Like, right now? What if a bunch of guys raped her …?" Let's answer Tosh's question quickly: It wouldn't be funny if that woman got raped by five guys. So why does the audience laugh? It's not that men are essentially jokey, high-fiving rapists. Instead, the laughter is the result of a larger structural problem (i.e., "rape culture") that allows for the patriarchal status quo to go unchallenged (or, at least, for its challenges to be the very thing that social codes of conduct, the "unwritten laws," are meant to suppress — since

---

[22] We'd like to acknowledge Kim O'Donnell here, who helped us break some of the ideas we're working through on the dangerous topic of the rape joke.

[23] While there are multiple versions of the unfilmed set, including assertions that Tosh was misquoted, we're following the woman's initial account, originally posted at http://breakfastcookie.tumblr.com/post/26879625651/so-a-girl-walks-into-a-comedy-club (accessed March 11, 2014).

"everyone knows" that it's all "just jokes" and, in the structure of the setting, the woman in the audience is supposed to find the idea of rape, like any idea presented by the man on stage, funny). In the context of the comedy club (where you go to laugh) and the ugly and discomforting irony of Tosh's boundary-pushing, there emerges a solidarity between men (and likely some women) akin to that in Freud's analysis. In a context like this, it becomes very plausible for victimization to turn funny as long as you're not the victim (or can't empathize fully). As Tosh castigates the woman who dares interrupt him, because she assumes both the role of the heckler *and* the role of the feminist killjoy, we can imagine the audience siding with him as the protector of their privileged good time. After all, they're only jokes.

It's also easy to see how Freud's model can be flipped by comedians, where the joke can be a kind of attack *as* critique depending on the power relations of those involved. Examples of this are as far-reaching as Dave Chappelle's explications of contemporary race relations or the self-critical reversals of Sarah Silverman and Louis C.K.[24] The political ugliness of the joke as an attack can be rerouted into critique as long as the parties involved are

---

[24] Sarah Silverman in particular likes to twist a joke through multiple offensive poses: "Everybody blames the Jews for killing Christ, and then the Jews try to pass it off on the Romans. I'm one of the few people that believe it was the blacks." Sarah Silverman, Jesus Is Magic (Interscope, 2005), DVD. It's worth pointing out that Silverman, like Tosh, thinks rape can be funny ... if the joke is that it's *not* funny. In a bit from her 2013 HBO special *We Are Miracles* about how she "need[s] more rape jokes," Silverman examines some of the complex power dynamics that come into play: "Rape jokes are great.

careful not to produce or reproduce (except perhaps iron-ically[25]) inequitable or hierarchical relations. In short, hu-mour provides an opportunity to ask how we might open up sites of resistance, providing opportunities to begin to rearticulate our social field. Avant-garde practice works similarly, aiming (as the military term *avant-garde* im-plies) to be at the forefront of artistic and social move-ments. Historically, avant-garde practice aligns itself with social change (for good or ill), attempting to bring art and everyday life together in a transformative way, allowing people to conceive of new ways to materially and collec-tively organize. Comedy shares with avant-garde practice this revolutionary potential, since both use techniques that can challenge, short-circuit, and alter dominant practices.

Or — and this is important — how comedy and the avant-garde *fail* to do this. Literature professor and poet

---

They make a comic seem so edgy and so dangerous, and the truth is it's like the safest area to talk about in comedy. Because who's gonna complain about a rape joke? I mean, I would say rape victims, but they're traditionally not complainers." Silverman develops the joke, pushing further while expanding the context to clarify her position: "I mean, the worst thing that can happen is someone comes up to you after a show and is like, 'Look, I'm a victim of rape, and I just want to say I thought that joke was insensitive and inappropriate and totally my fault and I am so sorry.'" Here the "joke" is that a rape joke re-victimizes the offended listener while securing the comic's sense of superiority — the rape joke as a sort of metaphorical rape. Sarah Silverman qtd. from a video in Rich Juzwiak, "Here Is Sarah Silverman's Rape Joke," *Gawker* (26 November 2013), available at http://gawker.com/here-is-sarah-silvermans-rape-joke-1472012603 (accessed March 11, 2014).

[25] But even then, the idea of an "ironic racism" or "ironic sexism" is problematic depending on who is making the joke and at whom the punchline aims.

Gregory Betts has argued for the use of the term *avant-garde* in its limited/historical context and has injected a cautionary politics and a much-needed historicity into poet Ron Silliman's term *post-avant*, while distinguishing experimental modes of contemporary poetry from modernist and postmodernist modes with radical or reactionary political agendas. It's a hoot! In other words, Betts argues that a belief in political progress through art is a defining characteristic of the avant-garde, but he suggests that much contemporary poetry is post-avant in that it shares many of the aesthetic qualities of avant-garde art as it has been traditionally defined but "without much tangible faith in progress or revolution."[26] Similarly, postmodern comedy often appears to waffle between these poles — between the conviction that it matters and the knowledge that it doesn't.

Hoping not so much to write Aristotle's missing book, we instead present *Why Poetry Sucks*[27] as our attempt at a grand PR stunt, parading out the participants in a literary world where the joke is suddenly something important, something that produces real effects. Rather than produce work that is too silly or jokey, the poets in *Why Poetry Sucks* draw from deep traditions in both poetry and comedy, often challenging the rigid literary and political im-

---

[26] Gregory Betts, *Avant-Garde Canadian Literature: The Early Manifestations* (Toronto: U of Toronto P, 2013), 20.

[27] An alternative title for the ideal Canadian anthology was suggested by Dave McGimpsey over Twitter: *Buick Presents: Better Than You!*

passes they encounter. We want to argue that, in our current social and cultural game of *Blockado* (the game of barricades), humour can act as an important sledge, taking a swing at the places and institutions we might wish changed, while acknowledging our apparent inability to change them.

When we began to gather material for this anthology, we planned a wider historical frame, considering the field of English-Canadian poetry starting with the first rumblings of postmodernism in the '60s. We saw in figures such as bpNichol, George Bowering, David W. McFadden, and Dennis Cooley a strong undercurrent that had wound its way into the writing of our contemporary moment. The project quickly became untenable, and not only because of our budget. What we didn't anticipate was the sheer amount of contemporary work that, in one way or another, picks up the legacy of poets like these, leading us to tighten our frame. The result is an anthology that loosely collects from the first decade and a half of the 21st century, with a knowledge that our collection is not a fixed whole but rather a sampling, complicated by bleeding edges and frayed threads. We have chosen to highlight a handful of poets and poems that cut across the spectrum of contemporary experimental work. Our aim is to showcase an array of both literary and comedic techniques by selecting poets less for their cultural presence or canonical heft than for how their poems exemplify some particular approach to experimentation-with-humour. We have included, where possible, multiple poems from each poet to give a sense of their general approach and style. What we haven't done is made a case for how *these* poets are *the* poets to pay attention to when it comes to humorous experimental poetry. We've opted for a cross-section and a snapshot, rather than issue some authoritative statement and feel quite confident we've missed something.[28]

Though we've drawn a line around a specific period, geography, and language, the poets here are most firmly drawn together by shared techniques and tactics, which can be defined by but are not limited to period, geography, genre, or medium. Each poet here operates amongst wider assemblages of texts, writers, politics, and power structures both inside and outside their immediate geographical and temporal spheres. These poets not only work within specific literary geographies but also exceed them, reading and working across national boundaries even as they work within them. They are likely to be influenced by George Bowering as much as Charles Bernstein, Russell Peters as much as Sarah Silverman, *SCTV* as much as *SNL*, or Ezra Levant as much as Bill O'Reilly. It's hard to imagine Stuart Ross' everyday surrealism without David W. McFadden on one side of the border and the New York School on the other. It's hard to imagine Susan Holbrook and Nicole Markotić's playful proceduralism without both the experiments of Oulipo and the serial punning of bpNichol. We originally planned to use the more specific (and, frankly, preferable) terms *avant-garde* and *post-avant* as Betts uses them, but, despite its horrors, the more

---

[28] Please text any complaints about the anthology or its inclusions to Aaron Giovannone, who has helpfully offered his cell phone number in one of the poems.

vague *experimental* does a better job of describing these disparate poems as a group (which experiment with form, play with convention, and otherwise tap into various subversive strains of literary history) and of simply communicating the thrust of the anthology without subjecting the works within to overly academic compartmentalizing.

Looking at humour and poetry together is a messy proposition, and we have decided to proceed messily. The poets collected here draw from deep wells that exceed poetry, moving into the worlds of stand-up and sitcoms, slapstick and pranks. They assert strong connections between poetry and comedy. We wish to assert that this connection is important, but it is not enough to simply say that poetry is funny and then point to funny poetry. We've asked why the connection is important and noted what is useful in the combination of poetry and humour, what led us to this soapbox we're standing on. We've noted what we see as the particular social and affective powers opened up in language by the joke and other comic techniques that draw poets and comedians to crack wise.

Only one more thing remains: Nacho Tuesdays.

In the comedy world, a distinction (however false) exists between comics who "work blue" and those who "work clean." Annharte opens the anthology with a slap in the face through the time-honoured tradition of toilet humour, the joke being how silly (and oppressive) it might be to find words obscene and taboo in the first place. Her experimentation often occurs in this realm, where she advances progressive politics but refuses the politically correct language with which it comes parcelled.

In "Squaw Guide," Annharte's form remains relatively conventional, but the pose of her speaker anticipates and subverts reader expectations. Shifting between the position of the comic and the heckler, Annharte often "sets up" a sentiment we might expect in a confessional lyric ("I don't have a closet / that's empty enough for me to get inside") and then spins into a punchline that turns the poem towards satire. Here, she explains the image ("think about it I got too many skeletons") the way you'd explain a joke to someone who just didn't "get it."

Annharte (a.k.a. Marie Baker) is Anishinabe (Little Saskatchewan First Nation, Manitoba) and lives in Winnipeg. She is the author of *Being on the Moon* (Polestar, 1990), *Coyote Columbus Café* (Moonprint, 1994), *Blueberry Canoe* (New Star, 2001), *Exercises in Lip Pointing* (New Star, 2003), *Indigena Awry* (New Star, 2012), and *AKA Inendagosekwe* (Capilano University Editions, 2013).

Cuntajunta

Cunt do it alone cunt topped up cuntalina flow up spine cunt drip drop that cunt let go smooth cunt silk hair leave it to the cuntman is a man obsessed by cuntology cuntrary to cunteraphobic afraid to say the word listen cuntajunta is only a meeting of the minds of cunts denounce a couple of cunts ago this damn cunt was saying I was a cunt like she wasn't or didn't carry hers cuntly crotched must swear bigtime cunt off you pig cunt right now cunta a cuntinent defined North American one cunt two cunt three cunt times four cunts gives all these cunts hanging around the cuntateria hoping for free cunt giveaway to be cuntinued

Squaw Guide

You Audience
Me Squaw
need to practise those lines
it is not the same as Tarzan Jane address
in the old movies
he yelled as he swung out holding his vine
dropped down to deliver commands
to Simba after bossing Cheeta all day

it's not exactly the same either
being called squaw
after going to a high school football game
coming home on the bus
this drunk white hosehead
yells out from the back
there's a squaw sitting up front
no not me — didn't look around — not me
because I grew semi-invisible
nobody noticed I was the only
invisible Indian
going to high school in the city
back in the '50s
unless there were lots even I didn't see

I needed the low self-esteem concept
to explain why nobody was on my side
why nobody told him I belonged
they were being good Canadians

nice he was racist & nice I was the squaw
it didn't make me act up like Jay Silverheels
as if I would speak up to joke
WHAT DO YO MEAN
WE WHITEBODY

I wasn't Tonto or tough enough
to defer say kemosabe
you had to be tough
a popular Indian Jack Jacobs
Blue Bomber football champion

Aw fuckem if they can't take a joke
a stand up comic would hit hard
in a comeback routine tell off heckler
hey bud you lost a right to get laid
in the westend or northend by a squaw

why not if Tarzan
makes Simba lie down when told
& Cheeta screams pointing to his butt

Ok okay now no more drudge grudge
I'm taking women studies
& that's tough
because I don't have a closet
that's empty enough for me to get inside
think about it I got too many skeletons
this closet is full
haven't counted inventory yet

them bones dem bones
dem shy bones
like the typical squaw in the old days
I was the shy kind
my best friend used to laugh
holding fingers fanned out
hiding her whole self
the big mouth
because it was hard to be a big squaw
big public squaw
I was too invisible to laugh out loud

in the university I go every day
during classes I transform
from text book squaw
who doesn't speak up
I usually do this
scary business when not supposed
to say anything contentious
silence is reward or reworded
everyone looks my way
to check if I am being quiet each day
I might abuse my feminism
switch bitch from academic squaw
to academic sasquatch

as I speak squaws are past tense
used to be but nobody says that word much

hey but wait a minute
did you gaze at me funny
intend just a bit
to call me a squaw?

being a squaw is very demanding
in the movies or on a native production set
it is when a woman gets told

> make tea squaw
> braid my hair after

said by a warrior no less

on the rez the women say my chief what my chief says
his speech never mentions my squaws my papooses
now why is that?

it's hard to be a political correct squaw
my secret: don't ever open mouth
or let yawn indicate how boring
better not to say anymore about that

but say the drunken squaw is aggressive best
saw some young women doing some reverse
squaw baiting
they were sitting in a bus shelter
whenever a guy would go by
one of them would say
HEY HUN-NAY
intimidating voice all husky
BOO JOO HUN-NAY

at next pow wow in South Dakota
I would say in breathy tone
WASHTE HUN-NAY

should feminism makes me too shy
to joke around much
them women now talk about outing
wonder out where?
in the bush?

probably out of my mind
like I said
dis closet is all junk
I'm serious
know all inside
intimate me squaw

Working out of a shared translation practice, Avasilichioaei and Moure dramatize a cycle of mistranslations of Romanian poet Nichita Stănescu inaugurated by translator-errant Elisa Sampedrín. First appearing in Moure's *Little Theatres* (Anansi, 2005), Sampedrín is Moure's heteronym (a pen name with a wildly different biography) whose writing practice consists of intervening in the texts of others. These interventions, the mistranslations and huffy retranslations that make up this sequence, compose a kind of heady prank (the sequence, collectively, is titled "Prank!") where, contrary to the idea that translation must display fidelity to the original, the translations refuse to behave.

The result is a mannered academic slapstick where Avasilichioaei and Moure frustratingly try to recover their composure and more accurately compose Stănescu's poem after Sampedrín monkeys with it. If the poem is a prank, our laughter comes from seeing attempt after attempt at accurate translation be foiled, with Avasilichioaei and Moure caught like millionaires in the middle of a *Three Stooges* pie fight, or heading back to the drawing board like Coyotes that can never quite catch Sampedrín's Road Runner.

Living in Montreal, Oana Avasilichioaei is the author of four books of poetry including *Abandon* (Wolsak and Wynn, 2005), *feria: a poempark* (Wolsak and Wynn, 2008), the co-written (with Erín Moure) *Expeditions of a*

Chimæra (BookThug, 2009), and *We, Beasts* (Wolsak and Wynn, 2012). She has translated the work of Romanian poet Nichita Stănescu, Québecoise poet Louise Cotnoir, and Québecois novelist and filmmaker Daniel Canty.

Also living in Montreal (but often seen elsewhere), Erín Moure is the author of seventeen books of poetry, most recently *The Unmemntioable* (Anansi, 2012), as well as a book of essays on poetic practice, *My Beloved Wager* (NeWest, 2009). She has translated or co-translated twelve books from writers such as Portuguese poet Fernando Pessoa, Québecoise poet and novelist Nicole Brossard, and Galician poets Chus Pato and Rosalía de Castro.

The Roost, *translated by E.S. from Nichita Stănescu*

1.
I was out in the field.
My pen stopped working.
I had to write with a straw.

2.
Where they'd torn up the rails
behind the sewing factory, I found a field.
In the field, when wind rises,
the grass clangs.

3.
I sat down on a concrete boulder in the field.
A mouse treads to the lip of its tunnel
and pushes my boot.

And the sky is a roost
for birds.

It appears that in the 1990s Elisa Sampedrín spent time in Romania, where she fell in with the poems of Nichita Stănescu and attempted, with no knowledge of Romanian, to translate them into English, which she was also unfamiliar with. The resulting debauchery was immediately, and later, unpublishable.

Now that Stănescu's poems have made a home in Canada in excellent English versions (*Occupational Sickness*, BuschekBooks, tr. Oana Avasilichioaei), it at last makes sense to unearth some of Sampedrín's poems.

Erín Moure, a Canadian poet who had previously endured Sampedrín's meddling in her own *Little Theatres*, has examined these translations in light of Sampedrín's known history, and insists it is impossible that they be hers.

We attribute them to her anyhow, believing Moure wrong in her archaeography.

About Sampedrín's attempts at translation, one critic wrote: "The line, the poetic line, confounds geometry. It becomes *lineage*, which is to say, older and younger at once."

Prajina/Cotețul, *restored to Romanian by O.A. from the English of E.S.*

1.

Eram pe teren.
Stiloul n-a mai vrut să scrie.
Am fost silită să scriu cu un pai.

2.

Unde au smuls șinele
în spate la fabrica de tricotaje, am găsit un câmp.
Pe câmp, când vântul se întețește,
iarba dangănă.

3.

M-am așezat pe un bolovan de beton în câmp.
Un șoarece pășește până la buza tunelului său
și-mi împinge cisma.

Și cerul e un coteț de vrăbii.

Because Elisa Sampedrín erroneously translated, in the previous
piece, a poem by Nichita Stănescu that had not been written in the
first place, Oana Avasilichioaei, Stănescu's Canadian translator, was
obliged to translate backward, and create the original Stănescu poem
we have here.

Coatful, *tr. E.S. from the Romanian of O.A*.

1.
I felt my foot.
Silhouette at the root of a scream.
Frost silting a scream with a stick.

2.
Where smoke signals
spit on the fabric of tractors, there's gas in a camp.
The camp's foot, when its vantage point interests you,
dangles grasses.

3.
Me, I'm seized up in camp, one foot a block of cement.
A soreness of pastures abuzz in the tarsal tunnel
till the chasm impinges.

I'm sealed in a coat of rage.

The problem with Avasilichioaei's translation backward in time into
the original Romanian of Sampedrín's translation entitled "The Roost"
is that it renders Sampedrín's purported translation *accurate*. And we
all know that Sampedrín does not know Romanian.

Fortunately, Sampedrín herself appears to have remedied this here,
by translating the now-original Romanian of Avasilichioaei-Stănescu.

Prank/1:45, *by E.M.*

1.

Put your best foot forward.
Stilettos in the hand are a kind of saw.
False stilettos, scraping the planks.

2.

You can make a small city
in a textile factory, cook with camp gas.
In the camp, a huge pot of intestines,
stirred with a spoon.

3.

Quick, put your foot in the door, and get your bets in.
Patience in tunnels makes the bones soar
over the abyss.

And the sky — a car crassh.

Maintaining her insistence that Sampedrín's translations are impossible, and are in fact not hers, Moure claims this to be the original poem, and refutes any resemblance to Stănescu's work, though allows for the possibility of coincidence between her original poem and Avasilichioaei's translation of the translation of Stănescu's poem. Avasilichioaei, for her part, asserts this to be an accurate translation into English of Stănescu's Romanian, and not an original poem as Moure claims. Avasilichioaei offers, in defense of her view, only that a car crash means a roost for birds.

Jocul/1:45, *tr. O.A. from the English of E.M.*

1.

Pune-ți piciorul perfect înainte.
În mână, tocurile cui sânt un fel de fierăstrău.
False, tocuri cui zgârie podeaua.

2.

Poți construi un mic oraș
într-o fabrica de tricotaje, găti la foc de tabără.
În tabără, o lingură amestecă
intestinele într-o oală uriașă.

3.

Grăbește-te, proptește piciorul în ușă, și pune pariu.
În tunele, răbdarea face oasele să zboare
deasupra abisului.

Și cerul — o bușitură de mașini.

Avasilichioaei distrusts the notion that an original ever existed or
could exist, but admits, when pressed, that a translation is an original,
and that she has access to the only true translation of Moure's poem,
which she attempts here to restore into the language of Stănescu. At
least we now have this original, and are relieved.

Jocularity #145, *tr. E.S. from the Romanian of O.A.*

1.

You put me in the perfect instant.
This morning my slipper with its saint felt, out the window.
False, the slipper with its egrarious footstep.

2.

Maybe you built a wee oar
in a text factory, the cat tiptoed on the table.
On the table, language mixed
intestinal between all that curiosity.

3.

Grab it, protest pictorial in america, if it so appears.
In a tunnel, rub faces with an oasis then soar
over the abyss.

And unruly — imagine it, ouch! The pop-rattle of machines.

The original of the copy is here originated in translation by Elisa
Sampedrín, who still does not know any Romanian but won't desist.
We don't know how E.S. got hold of the work of O.A., unless she
found it in a book by Stănescu, where it hadn't, at that moment, been
written. Yet the unruliness has a ring of truth to it, and it cuts to the
bone.

If the Shoe Fits, Scare It. *a revision of Jocularity #145 by E.S.*

1.
You put me in the perfect instant.
I felt my foot.
My slipper with its saint felt, out the window.

2.
Foolish, the slipper with its egregious footstep,
a wee oar out of a text factory.
On the table, language mixed
intestinal between all that curiosity,
no wonder the cat tiptoes,
silhouette at the root of a scream.

3.
And the sky rose — a car crassh.

It is not clear here why Sampedrín felt compelled to revise "Jocular-
ity." As far as we can assess there was no need for such a revision.
However, scribbled in the margin of Sampedrín's notebook on the
page where this poem is penned, we found this: "a rose is a rose is a
rose is not repetition."

Felt Hat Now, *tr. E.S. from the English of E.M.*

1.
Stilettos in the hand are as good as a saw.
She can tunnel in sore bones
while the chasm impinges.
Quick, put her foot in the door,

get my bets in.

2.
You could magnetize salt.
With your pulse I'm perfectly inane.
The tongue's just the far
end of the intestine, they're both

unruly, and what tunnels between:
sly passersby leap facing the abyss.

And the foot is the head — where's my felt hat now?

"We refute, we refute, we refute."
"What exactly?"
"This act, which makes the mouth hurt."
(Scribbled into the margins of Sampedrín's notebook.)

I inverted it.
I had to sit on a pen and write with a rock.
The crashing sky my roost.

3.
Language of translation
roots in the factory textiling text.
Railway tracks cross uncross this junction.
Dangling legs over a cliff's abyss, children are innocent.

2.
In the perfect instant language is a bridge.
You on the bridge
bird-soaring.

1.
Are we game?

The sole poem worth reading in the original appears to be this one, a gaming lesson, by Oana Avasilichioaei. The rest of the poem is a prank.

Working from a series of procedural constraints, whether loosely repeating a word (as in the poem "Nails") or constructing rigorous anagrams, Elizabeth Bachinsky draws humour from the generative materiality of language. In the two poems from her book *The Hottest Summer in Recorded History*, Bachinsky repeats words ("NAILS") and syntax ("And who"; "And where") to create excessive chains of shifting details.

In "Lead the Wants," Bachinsky takes a different, stricter approach, anagrammatically translating each line of T.S. Eliot's "The Waste Land" to produce a much different poem that anticipates American poet K. Silem Mohammad's similar treatment of Shakespeare's sonnets in *The Sonnagrams*. In Bachinsky's rewriting of Eliot, the opening line "April is the cruellest month, breeding" becomes "Brilliant duel them corset her penis." Near the end of the excerpt here, Bachinsky buries a mocking apology/homage: "O, Eliot — dead — this wound an offer. Thanks."

Elizabeth Bachinsky lives in Vancouver and is the author of five books of poetry, most recently *I Don't Feel So Good* (BookThug, 2012) and *The Hottest Summer in Recorded History* (Nightwood, 2013). She is the editor of *EVENT* magazine.

Nails

for Danielle Devereaux

I'm looking for a place that's just called NAILS.
There's always some place that's just called NAILS.
In every city and suburb, they'll do your NAILS.
They don't do waxing. All they do is NAILS.
Doesn't look fancy. Smells like NAILS.
Not a spa. No massage. Just your NAILS.
A gal talks smack while she files your NAILS
as the rain comes down outside like NAILS
on the roof of this place that's just called NAILS.
(You're in good hands. Just look at her NAILS!)
Where the working girls go to get their NAILS.
Where the travellers go to get their NAILS.
Have you seen this place? It's just called NAILS.
There's a neon light outside. Says NAILS.

I Want to Have a Chuck and Di Party Like My Parents Did in the '80s

for Jamella Hagen

But where will I get the helicopter?
And who will make my dress
out of garbage bags for me? And where
will I find the two-by-four and a good-sized
rock for our game of rockball?
And how will we climb the ridge
to the glacier? And who will dig
the trench to the fuel pump? And where
will we get the klieg lights? And who
will decorate the army cots
with fluorescent tape? And which forest
might accommodate us? And who's got
a big enough van? And who'll bring
the eucalyptus? And which river will
be cold enough? And where will we get
the lumber? And who knows how to build
a sauna? And how long will it take to grow
our beards? And who's got a canoe?
And who can lift it into the helicopter? And
how will it fit? And who can fly the helicopter?
And then what will we do with it?
What about the caribou and the siksiks?
We'll need a rifle just in case. Last year there
was a grizzly bear. Last year there
was no night. Last year we got in trouble.

Last year we wore hula skirts. Last year
we lost Arden, then found her. Last
year we looked through binoculars. Last
year the kids played in the iron tailings.
Last year Frankie blew up the pumphouse.
Let's not do that again! Let us not eat
Wonder Bread, let's eat bannock.
Let's eat ham with scalloped potatoes
and also some of that saskatoon berry jam.
Let's cook with mom in the trailer.
Let's swing from the beams in the bunkhouse.
Let's hold the fossils the geologists found.
Let's hold the geologists. O, white night
of northern remembering, let your still light fall
on the faces of your partiers. The elders say
the sun is not coming up where it should.
What does this mean for meteorologists?
What does this mean for us?

[from] Lead the Wants

Pardon our fez
Foil rim broil bag

1. Ribald Teeth of Bead

Brilliant duel them corset her penis.
A million toxic duds dangle. Get a
Night-rise or day-rites — merge, mend.
Withstand null grip or *soir*.
We saw murder in it. Veto kept
Slough for wine — a ten cent ring.
Dried, brittle, few fillies that
Murmur homage on Rubens' trees disperse rug-covers — those
Clowns! What death sheer torpor paid to a waif on
The run. What neon cadet lit nine gone gifts? None.
An anathema of need, our offer lacked
Stamina, snarl. Deadening, the unseen music dug kitsch
Instead. Her brine-randy nukes were arched (whack!)
And look guilty. Who's she on? *Et tu*, commie?
It's a night friend, a washed mare, said e.
E might tow on the wed old air-wand
I tread. Nigh in ten and no one fights worth much.

Such great clout. What a hoot! Water arcs, hewn
From this bout of thin youth *sans* runs. Bob,
He's a wooly sort of noun. Go on you Yank.
Magic bracken tears us. Here he abets us hop anew.
Send the RV on the loch. Seek life, dread ice. Teeter, Tern. Fight.

One fond day there was no loud Troy,
No woken Thunder's redress hit hard C
Or redid work. Thin came the sound of she.
Wilting candy for thou, friend: ether. How lissome. I'm
Gone. If stars hid on you I'd turn — wag my hind orb.
Fill in your sudden Iowa awash until off

> *He winds with Fred,*
> *Her much dear zit,*
> *Rich in kids.*
> *Mine? Lest I'd wow u.*

O Hymen cave a fist. Youth is a gray gear.
They chill. That iced hymen. Real.
Tactile. Rome began a feather, waged hymen.
Our tiny new land — sacked. Her, truly warm. Oh, if you ouch,
Say yes. I clean mail with soft dander. Peek
In. Dig in. Knead what gone *noir*
There dances. Love. Oh, oh — King of nine little gilt t.
Dun deer lead so mere.

Damascus so sofa it envoy or lariat.
Them never bless cold dada ham.
The nine bone town is woe. Me? Art-whisk soup.
What a picked shark hears as cow fed dice.
Phone a druid; record a snail. I throw one's icy
Theory as trash. Please, eerie stew? Look
A bell! Hey, don't shade the locks for a rein
Says the lad of tuition.
Heh … what sheer investment we hilt a tree he adheres

Tire his dear crone's hand yet heed me and chant
Kiss me hibiscus, eschew an albino, nick the high arrow.
Bid choirs do infinite monad dots. Wife,
Heat me new. Fan better hardy had hag.
Nearing grown pie, encoded leak, roof slip
And/or rank equity (IOU these). You fee me.
I'm shy. The e felt horror. Sing, *belle*. Cop
A colt no sty refuses (me). Behead us.

Lure a tiny c
Down the roof. Awning water bred fun
And flowers, some clover, a boon (dowdy) Ding!
This yeoman thought one hound hadn't a dad,
Nor quest, when green firs dated rash helix.
Lilliputian world, mow the lawn. Shed, dine — Get
What pink May flowers the sour north took thee.
O, Eliot — dead — this wound an offer. Thanks.
No, no. That's kryptonite's menacing hiss newer den wiped.
Thou many rosehips, we tale, we they, whim I.
Yes, trader, you plant a corpulent daisy hat goner.
Has it begun to sprout? Will it bloom this year?
Don't be fast, udder-horses dish buttes rid.
Mention to her fresh fence kept at godhead.
Some turn hyperbolic near our left emblem, coy e.

GARY BARWIN

Drawing from a well of melancholy, these poems from Gary Barwin's *The Porcupinity of the Stars* perform a kind of soft surrealism, mapping flights of fancy on the everyday. "Psalm" couples a sad tone with images of consumer culture and references to '70s television (including *The Brady Bunch* and *The Partridge Family*), producing a static snow between the guffawing and weeping that accompanies cultural recognition. "Comedy" works similarly, pairing apocalyptic imagery with domestic appointment ("eat a bomb, sure / but meet your sweetie for dinner"). Are we meant to ask whether, for Barwin, comedy is this kind of incursion into our blasé patterns, a real thing that can upturn our lives with the ease of the projected light of the situation comedy? How close is comedy to crying?

Gary Barwin is a writer, composer, multimedia artist, educator, and performer. His recent books include *The Porcupinity of the Stars* (Coach House Books, 2010), the co-written (with Hugh Thomas and Craig Conley) *Franzlations: The Imaginary Kafka Parables* (New Star, 2011), the co-written (with Gregory Betts) *The Obvious Flap* (BookThug, 2011), and *Moon Baboon Canoe* (Mansfield, 2014). Recordings of his work can be found at PennSound. He lives at garybarwin.com and in Hamilton, Ontario.

Psalm

By the late-night pickup window, we sat and wept
when we remembered ourselves

We hung our TVs upon the air in the midst thereof

For there our captors required of us songs
they that seized us, required of us joy
saying, "Sing us one of the songs of Keith"

How shall we sing Danny's song in a strange land?

If I forget thee, O Chris and freedom
may my right hand forget how to make dog shadows by lamplight

If I do not remember thee, Tracy and peacetime
may my tongue cling to the roof of the bus as it goes on tour
if I prefer not Laurie and justice above my chief joy

Remember, O Keith, what Carol and Mike did
in the days of fire
who said, "Tear them down. Tear them down. Tear them down!"

O de facto American children, doomed to destruction,
happy is he who repays you

He who taketh and dasheth your babies
against the screen

Comedy

go to sleep
then get up again

be crucified
then rise

eat a bomb, sure
but meet your sweetie for dinner

I let the dragon into the house
and it burns both piano and shoes

our home is an ashen cloud with an incomprehensible address
barefoot, we walk to the store for ice cream

slip on a moose

Relieving

Daddy said
Son you have to make your own dog
if you have none

and I said
I have a fire hydrant
so I can just imagine

Although conceptual poetry has a reputation for being *especially* unfunny (even though the concepts involved are often obvious jokes that its critics just don't "get"), derek beaulieu's "January 28, 1986" discovers black comedy in an unlikely historical moment: the *Challenger* disaster. This transcribed dialogue, from a home video taken during the event, lacks the tragic tone of Kenneth Goldsmith's transcription of news reports of the same disaster (see Goldsmith's *Seven American Deaths and Disasters*) and instead resembles the comic dialogue of a Warner Bros. cartoon.

"Nothing Odd Can Last" takes a variation of Samuel Johnson's famous dismissal of Laurence Sterne's experimental novel *The Life and Opinions of Tristram Shandy, Gentleman* as its title. ("Nothing odd will do for long. *Tristram Shandy* did not last.") beaulieu then reproduces reader discussion questions from Coles Notes style websites, proof that the novel *has* lasted. The poem works both as a refutation to Johnson and (more pointedly) a tongue-in-cheek rebuke to contemporary criticisms of conceptual poetry. The appreciative discussion questions, which are as vapid as Johnson's complaint, are also the targets of the satire, so the poem, oddly, functions as a *better* criticism of conceptual poetry than the standard critiques, warning that conceptual poetry's apparent radicality is in danger of domestication through debased academic discourse.

derek beaulieu is the author or editor of fifteen books, most recently *Writing Surfaces: The Selected Fiction of John Riddell* (co-edited with Lori Emerson) (Wilfrid Laurier UP, 2013) and *Please, No More Poetry: The Poetry of derek beaulieu* (edited by Kit Dobson; Wilfrid Laurier UP, 2013). He is the publisher of No Press and is the visual poetry editor at UbuWeb. beaulieu has exhibited his work in galleries across Canada, the U.S., and Europe. He currently teaches at the Alberta College of Art + Design.

January 28, 1986

There's George. Where does she come up, George? Yeah, but where does it come up? I think you need to be over there. There it goes. I see it in between the trees. There it is coming right over top the trees. Uh huh it be right on top of those trees. I saw it. There it goes. That's brighter than usual. Yeah. It is. Oh yeah. Right over those trees. I saw it when it went through that hole. I don't remember it being that bright, that big. Me neither. What was that part? It must be part of one of them boosters. Oh look, there's two. It's going off into two. That trouble or not? They're not having trouble, are they? That's trouble some kind, George. That's trouble of some kind, innit it or not? There it goes again. I think I'll go in and listen. They got troubles. No, that's trouble of some kind, George. That's trouble of some kind. That doesn't look right. Yeah, I haven't either. It's not as bad as it was. I don't know, it sure didn't look right. It what? Exploded? What? Said it exploded? Boy, I knew it didn't look right. You could tell. There's some trouble all right. That's sorta a historical moment we got here on tape I guess. Hope we got it on tape, let's see what happens.

Nothing Odd Can Last

Are the bawdy passages and double entendres important in this book?

Could it have been omitted?

Does the author guide his pen or does his pen guide him?

Does she have redeeming qualities?

Does the novel demonstrate that there can be postmodern texts before post-modernism?

Do you think the author intended to end the novel with the ninth volume?

How do we account for the author's strikingly unsentimental treatment, at times, of such topics as love and death?

How does the seventh volume, in which the narrator describes his travels through Europe, relate to the rest of the book?

How ironical is their presentation?

How much control do you think the writer has over the mixture of digression — both kinds mentioned above — and the narrator's history?

How sentimental and gushy is the writer of this book?

If the latter is true, what justification can there be for that?

If you were a reader like the Lady, who reads "straight forwards, more in quest of the adventures, than of the deep erudition and knowledge," how would you feel about the novel?

In what way are such details important to the author's method?

In what way is it possible to reconcile the statement that the book will "be kept a-going" for forty years with the contention that the novel is completed?

Is it legitimate for an author to require — or even request — that the reader do things like "imagine to yourself," replace misplaced chapters, and put up with omitted chapters?

Is kindheartedness necessarily mawkishness?

Is she as stupid as she seems?

Is the author in control of his digressions (and merely affecting their spontaneity), or does the story actually run away from him and have to be reined back in?

Is the writer unable to present a straightforward story, or does he deliberately frustrate the reader?

Is there any importance to this, or is it just the author's bawdiness?

Is there sufficient justification for such passages in the book?

Or should the reader say to heck with it?

What are some of the qualities that the writer of the book has inherited from his forebears?

What does this indicate about the writer's plan and his control of what he was doing?

What evidence is there that the narrator's childhood traumas actually influence his adult personality?

What is the author's attitude toward science?

What is the effect of the precise visual details given in the book?

What is the effect of the narrator's frequent addresses to his audience?

What is the relationship between the "I" who narrates the story and the author?

What kinds of scenes receive this treatment?

Which predominates?

Why or why not?

Would it make sense to interpret the novel psychoanalytically?

Would you argue for or against his statement?

Would you rather that they were deleted from it?

Stemming from a practice of collecting and compiling found textual material, the poems in Gregory Betts' *This is Importance* are composed of material mined from student assignments and exams. Full of misunderstanding and malapropism, the students' lines are individually funny because of the way they stumblingly resist our standard understandings of the material they are meant to make instrumental.

On one level, the plundered material smacks of the smug practice of posting material like this on Facebook or Twitter ("Hey, check out these *idiots!*"), but Betts both emulates and exceeds that kind of snarky dismissal by choosing material that doesn't merely misunderstand but also accidentally critiques the institutional goals of the university. Often, despite apparent lack of any such intentions, the lines appear like witty barbs ("It is marginal to find a voice in Canada" sounds like the kind of complaint a snarky reviewer might make) or suggest some deeper, sly comprehension ("Margaret Atwood's theory of survival barely applies to her own writing"). Betts charts the moments where quantifiable research and reasoned argument slides into a different kind of knowledge production: poetry.

Gregory Betts is the author of five books of poetry, editor of five books of experimental Canadian writing, and author of *Avant-Garde Canadian Literature: The Early Manifestations* (U of Toronto P, 2013). His most recent book is *This is Importance: A Students' Guide to Literature* (Wolsak and Wynn, 2013), a compilation of student errors. He teaches Canadian and avant-garde literature and is the director of the Centre for Canadian Studies at Brock University in St. Catharines, Ontario.

Canadian Literature: The Confederation Era

At the turn of the twentieth century, writers were a minority amongst Canadian writers.

It is marginal to find a voice in Canada.

Technological advances, such as the printing press, had an impact on the books by Bliss Carmen, Archibald Lampmen, Charles Roberts and Duncan Scott.

Both Roberts and Carman are places themselves within the landscape.

Although many authors are fictional, Margaret Atwood says that many carry a "Canadian" tone. The characters suffer for this.

Before Confederation, the First World War took refuge in the Canadian wilderness. The First World War was one of many battles taking place at the time. Nature was Canada's best technology.

We experience the wild, they experienced the wilderness.

Canada is lacking animals because of their depiction in poetry.

Contemporary Canada

There was a literal explosion in Canadian literature after 1950.

Patrick Lane describes four different things that Canadian literature falls on.

Robert Kroetsch uses imagery because he is a poet in love with a painter.

Margaret Atwood

Canadian tales are always traumatic experiences. See, for instance, Margaret Atwood.

I tried to use the Post Structure to build my argument about Margaret Atwood.

Atwood is typical of the narrator who knows little and experiences even less. Her characters are confused about their point.

The poetry of Margaret Atwood and Alfred Purdy share the same similarities.

Both Atwood and Purdy frequently use death as a symbol of the inability to survive.

Margaret Atwood's theory of survival barely applies to her own writing.

Atwood's protagonists often lack the female body.

Margaret Atwood used settings in, not just her poems, but her novels as well.

Margaret Atwood uses mages of nature throughout her poetry.

As a foreigner, Margaret Atwood does not understand Canada.

Atwood gives freedom to her readers by confusing them. In fact, the narrator does this work for her.

Atwood is able to get across the stereotypes that come with being Canadian, such as Rednecks. By writing this, she is able to express our nation to others who may not believe her.

Offred throws up herself into the hands of the resistance.

Offred enters the flashback scene from the future. There she discovers what she already knew.

Offred is some kind of sexy, but not the pleasing kind. She is more like a narrative function.

She lives in a place that restricts women's right to speak for a long time. Therefore, she communicates through the male gaze.

Kat, in "Hairball," has an identity that lives in the sphere of consumer culture. She had it surgically removed.

Atwood bares her victimization, but Munro survives the experience.

Canadians are victimized by having to fight Margaret Atwood for survival.

Canadians paint the theme "survival" onto their books.

CHRISTIAN BÖK

An oddity of poetry readings is that material that can seem arch or academic on the page often comes across as loose and funny when read aloud. One thing that critics of *Eunoia* commonly overlook (aside from the fact that it accomplishes almost everything critics say it doesn't) is its comic qualities. Even though Bök goes out of his way to name-drop Snoop Dogg, the book gets misread as ultra-serious. Moreover, especially when read aloud, it's often hilarious (Bök's own performances often emphasize this, and if he ever flubs a word, it's because he laughed).

In "Chapter U," Bök plays with the absurd sonic atmosphere that results from the guttural repetitions due to the constraint of writing a univocalic lipogram (where the only vowel allowed is *u*). Ubu (a character from Alfred Jarry's play *Ubu Roi*) and his pursuit of hedonistic pleasure is, in its own way, an epic struggle. A clown, Ubu bungles through feasts and orgies in slapstick fashion, until he gets kung-fu punched by a bunch of Ku Klux Klan members — a scene that would fit right into a Will Ferrell movie.

Christian Bök, a professor of English at the University of Calgary, is the author of *Crystallography* (Coach House Press, 1994) and *Eunoia* (Coach House Books, 2001). He has created artificial languages for two television shows (Gene Roddenberry's *Earth: Final Conflict* and Peter Benchley's *Amazon*), earned praise for his sound poetry performances (particularly the *Ursonate* by Kurt

Schwitters), and crafted conceptual artworks (including books built out of Rubik's Cubes and Lego bricks). He is currently working on *The Xenotext Experiment*, an attempt to implant a poem into the DNA of an extremophilic bacteria, with the goal of writing a text that will survive to the end of the universe.

Chapter U

for Zhu Yu

Kultur spurns Ubu — thus Ubu pulls stunts. Ubu shuns *Skulptur*: Uruk urns (plus busts), Zulu jugs (plus tusks). Ubu sculpts junk *für Kunst und Glück*. Ubu busks. Ubu drums drums, plus Ubu strums cruths (such hubbub, such ruckus): *thump*, *thump*; *thrum*, *thrum*. Ubu puns puns. Ubu blurts untruth: much bunkum (plus bull), much humbug (plus bunk) — but trustful schmucks trust such untruthful stuff; thus Ubu (cult guru) must bluff dumbstruck numbskulls (such chumps). Ubu mulcts surplus funds (trust funds plus slush funds). Ubu usurps much usufruct. Ubu sums up lump sums. Ubu trumps dumb luck.

Duluth dump trucks lurch, pull U-turns. Such trucks dump much undug turf: *clunk, clunk — thud*. Scum plus crud plugs up ducts; thus Ubu must flush such sulcus ruts. Sump pumps pump: *chuff, chuff*. Such pumps suck up mush plus muck — dung lumps (plus clumps), turd hunks (plus chunks): grugru grubs plus fungus slugs mulch up humus pulp. Ubu unplugs flux. Ubu scrubs up curbs; thus Ubu must brush up sulfur dust plus lugnut rust: *scuff, scuff*. Ubu burns unburnt mundungus. Ubu lugs stuff; Ubu tugs stuff. Ubu puts up fulcrums. Ubu puts up mud huts, but mugwumps shun such glum suburb slums. *tut, tut*.

Dutch smut churns up blushful succubus lusts; thus buff hunks plus hung studs must fuck lustful sluts: Ruth plus Lulu. Ubu struts. Ubu snuffs up drugs. Ubu hugs Ruth; thus Ruth purrs. Ubu untucks Ruth's muumuu; thus Ruth must untruss Ubu's tux. Ubu fluffs Lulu's tutu. Ubu cups Lulu's dugs; Ubu rubs Lulu's buns; thus Lulu must pull Ubu's pud. Ubu sucks Ruth's cunt; Ubu cuffs Ruth's butt. Ubu stuffs Ruth's bum (such fun). Ubu pumps Lulu's plush, sun-burnt tush. Ubu humps Lulu's plump, upthrust rump. Ubu ruts. Ubu huffs; Ubu puffs. Ubu blurts: *push*, *push*. Ubu thrusts. Ubu bucks. Cum spurts. Ubu cums.

Ubu gulps up brunch: duck, hummus, nuts, fugu, bulgur, buns (crusts plus crumbs), blutwurst, brüh-wurst, spuds, curds, plums: *munch, munch*. Ubu sups. Ubu slurps rum punch. Ubu chugs full cups (plus mugs), full tubs (plus tuns): *glug, glug*. Ubu gluts up grub; thus Ubu's plump gut hurts. Ubu grunts: *ugh, ugh* Ubu burps up mucus sputum. Ubu up-chucks lunch. Ubu slumps. Ubu sulks. Ubu shrugs. Ubu slurs drunk chums. Ubu snubs such drunks; thus curt churls cuss: "shut up, Ubu, shut up." Gruff punks club Ubu. Butch thugs drub Ubu. Ku-klux cults kung-fu punch Ubu. Rumdum bums bust up pubs.

Gulls churr: *ululu, ululu*. Ducks cluck. Bulls plus bucks run thru buckbrush; thus dun burrs clutch fur tufts. *Ursus* cubs plus *Lupus* pups hunt skunks. Curs skulk (such mutts lurk: *ruff, ruff*). Gnus munch kudzu. Lush shrubs bud; thus church nuns pluck uncut mums. Bugs hum: *buzz, buzz*. Dull susurrus gusts murmur hushful, humdrum murmurs: *hush, hush*. Dusk suns blush. Surf lulls us. Such scuds hurl up cumulus suds (*Sturm und Druck*) — furls unfurl: *rush, rush*; curls uncurl: *gush, gush*. Such tumult upturns unsunk hulls; thus gulfs crush us, *gulp*, dunk us — burst lungs succumb.

LOUIS CABRI

Working at the level of the syllable, these poems from Louis Cabri's *Poetryworld* bend words and phrases out of shape, creating threads of mutating language. The humour comes out of repetitions that produce slight variations or weird combinations. On one level, we laugh at the strange sounds generated through the transformation, recombination, and mutation of the words. On another level, especially in "An Alphabet of Canada's Changing Role in Global Supply Chains of Syllables," these mutations act on a larger social stage as the names of provinces take on corporate qualities. The surface absurdity suggests a sad depth, since Alberta might as well call itself "AlbecCo."

Cabri's poems provoke laughter at the place where the materiality of language meets its social construction, by estranging language from its "natural" usage to abstract it to a point where it might ironically do a better job of describing social/political/economic realities.

Louis Cabri is the author of *The Mood Embosser* (Coach House Books, 2001) and *Poetryworld* (Capilano University Editions, 2010). He works at the University of Windsor. He was an organizer of the poets' talk series PhillyTalks in Philadelphia in the late '90s and early 2000s and, more recently, has been a co-organizer of the I'm in You, You're in Me talk series at Vancouver's Kootenay School of Writing.

An Alphabet of Canada's Changing Role in Global Supply Chains of Syllables

AlbecCo

Briber Dorbaanda

Labraland

Mabrunlumisle

New Edri

Newfoundta

Northka Swicklumbiries

Nukontchew

Onnatero

Prince Nito Ritor

Quéta

Sastishvutwan

Yuwest

"Place where trees stand in water" (Natural Resources Canada)

doer rah co.'s
d'or runt ant out

drawn to
Tron 2

to run in to
Taiwan too

'ti wren doc's
torrent Dow

tyrant dough
do-run do

do run tore
"d'oh!" a toe

dour end oh
tour wrong? no

tire on to
tie one on to

two wan tones
door in tow

to rant owe
two-rent toll

dirempt ho!
tong-raw tongue

tung ung. ta —
Tonto

to John Todd O
TO

Versa

ness
sun
n

'ee
is
a

pnyx
son
neeze

un
nice
unne

pneo
sign
ease

onde
lease
and

needs
hand
knees

on
gneiss
sand

ye
isse
san

kneads
anise
sound

-ness
and-
ni!

iss
an
innocent

nese
end
niece

any
sani
zani

lees
sang
-ies

Andes
sa'
Nissan fairy ann

Lindsay Cahill

Evoking the jokier side of the Internet's underbelly, Lindsay Cahill's poems arrange plundered material from *The Simpsons* into remixes centered around specific characters or motifs. The result is a hybrid of lyric poetry and Internet forum, complete with incessant *Simpsons* references ("with the kicking and the biting and the metal teeth and the hurting"). While a certain amount of humour comes from the simple referencing of familiar material (think of *Airplane*, *Hot Shots*, and *Scary Movie,* all movies whose humour depends on reproducing scenes from other movies), Cahill adds a layer of compositional cleverness in the way she frames the material she collects. In "drunk as a poet on payday," she organizes quotations from *The Simpsons* that reference the literary, collecting a specific sample to examine the way that the idea of the literary is joked about.

Cahill's work allows us to reflect on why the familiar is so funny — why does merely quoting *The Simpsons* generate a laugh? — but her reframing of this familiar material also produces new laughs out of new combinations *and* provides a space to consider the repeated patterns across a body of work.

Lindsay Cahill is a Toronto-based editor, visual poet, and remixer. Her work has appeared in *The Rusty Toque*, *Stroboscope*, and *The Volta*. She is the founding editor of *dead (g)end(er)* magazine and currently co-edits the Toronto- and NYC-based magazine *outlandish* with Kelly Wydryk.

46 72 69 6E 6B 20 72 75 6C 65 73 21

let's say we amscray outta here,
and have a wild wingding at the
Cyclotron, huh, doctor? —
ng heyyy,
            bwa haiiii.
oh, the colours, children!

mwaha, *weh*, all right —
just stay calm, Frinky ...
these babies will be in the stores
while he's still grappling
with the pickle matrix — *wha hooo.*
now that is some clever *vhyving*,
for crying out *flayven!*

and suppose we extend the square
beyond the two dimensions of our universe
along the hypothetical Z axis
via the concaaavity of that
oversized beverage conveyance
forming a three-dimensional object
known as a 'cube' ...
or, a 'Frinkahedron' — *mwa haiiii*,
oh, why, it should be obvious to even
the most dim-witted individual who holds an
advanced degree in hyperbolic topology,
thermodynamics, hyyypermathematics, and,
of course,

microcalifragalistics
that all robots will eventually turn against their masters
and run amok in an orgy of blood
with the kicking and the biting
and the metal teeth and the hurting
and the shoving and the running
and the exploding and the crying
and the grabbing
and the duct-taping
and the tennis ball in the mouth
and the truncheons with the acting
and the groupies and the "Luke, Luke, save me"
with the lightsaber and the *vwing, vwing, vwing*
and the wrathfulness and the vengeance
and the bloodrain and the
"hey hey hey, it hurts me" …

oh boy,

that monkey is going to pay …

drunk as a poet on payday

Pablo Neruda said that laughter is the language of the soul …
I know — I am familiar with the works of Pablo Neruda,
and, as your president, I would demand a science-fiction library
with an A-B-C of the genre: Asimov, Bester, Clarke …
but, no Ray Bradbury …

it's the Lisa Simpson Book Club —
Poe, Ginsberg, Kerouac.
those are my only friends —
grown-up nerds like Gore Vidal,
and even he's kissed more boys than I ever will …
but solitude never hurt anyone:
Emily Dickinson lived alone,
and she wrote some of the most
beautiful poetry the world has ever known …
then went crazy as a loon.

it was Mrs. Bouvier, y'know, who drove her friends,
Zelda Fitzgerald and Sylvia Plath, so crazy
with jealousy over her good looks;
but, don't be bashful. when I was your age,
kids made fun of me because I read at the ninth-grade level.
although, I hardly consider *A Separate Peace* the ninth-grade
     level …
pssht, more like pre-school.
it's the Ayn Rand School for Tots
where A is A, and Helping is Futile.
and I'd just like to remind you that Shirley Jackson's

"The Lottery"
does not contain any hints on how to win the lottery —
it is rather a chilling tale of conformity gone mad …

the turkey's a little dry?
the turkey's a little dry!
oh, foe, the cursed teeth!
what demon from the depths of hell created thee!

truth is beauty; beauty, truth, sir!
but, the truth can be harsh and disturbing —
how can that be considered beautiful?
oh, damn you, Walt Whitman —
damn-you-Walt-freaking-Whitman!
leaves of green, my ass!

goodbye, Springfield —
from hell's heart
I stab at thee.

The Krustiest Place On Earth

Urgent call for Mr. Clown,
there's a Krisis at Kamp Krusty —
oy gevalt! to the hydrofoil!
shut-up and eat your pinecone:
the exclusive program of diet and ridicule.
ah, the bucolic splendours of
an abandoned mule cannery
turned Dickensian workhouse:
9 out of 10 orphans can't tell the difference.

Size. Strength. Agility.

much obliged, doll, for your implements of destruction —
a group of school-aged Spartacuses
have taken the camp by force.

burn, Krusty, burn —
his autobiography was self-serving
with many glaring omissions,
but he's gonna bring us food,
and water,
and smite our enemies.
why, I haven't seen such unfettered
hurly burly since The Fall of Saigon.
now the effort of writing has made me lightheaded,
so I close by saying, *Save us!*
Save us now!

it's going to be a D-lightful summer.

Taking the form of a children's book of verse, Stephen Cain's *I Can Say Interpellation* produces a short-circuit between the seemingly innocuous realm of children's poetry and the subversive goals of Continental philosophy. What results in a poem like "ABC: An Amazing Alphabet Book!" is a clash between form and content as the complex critiques of Marx or Kristeva or Foucault are reduced to blips in an alphabetic catalogue: "F is for Foucault who wrote *The Order of Things.*" Both forms are connected to pedagogical practices — either early parental interaction ("What's this? What's this?") or the neoliberal training of the university ("Why *this?* Why *this?*"). Cain registers a goofy discomfort with the reduction of a rich critical apparatus to the instrumentality of making sure your kid will be employable in the future, while simultaneously displaying an obvious example of children's literature as an attempt at childhood interpellation, teaching children to reproduce the world in certain ways.

Stephen Cain is the author of *I Can Say Interpellation* (BookThug, 2011) and three earlier poetry collections — *American Standard/Canada Dry* (Coach House Books, 2005), *Torontology* (ECW, 2001), and *dyslexicon* (Coach House Books, 1998). He has also composed a collaborative series of micro-fictions, *Double Helix* (Mercury, 2006), with Jay MillAr, and co-authored, with Tim Conley, *The Encyclopedia of Fictional and Fantastic Languages* (Greenwood, 2006). He is the former literary editor of the *Queen Street Quarterly* and former fiction editor at Insomniac Press. He lives in Toronto, where he teaches avant-garde and Canadian literature at York University.

ABC: An Amazing Alphabet Book!

A is for Althusser
B is for Barthes
C is for Capital
D for Descartes

E is for Eliot's mermaid that sings
F's for Foucault who wrote *The Order of Things*

G is for Gramsci who in prison still wrote a book
H is for Hegel who's well worth a look

Ideology begins with I
Jouissance is J
K is for Kristeva on L, or Linguistics,
(Which is also Lacan's way)

M is for Marx who put workers ahead
N is for Nietzsche who said god is dead

O is an Object and
P is Plato's Perfection
Q stands for Query
And R's the Reflection

S is for Said
Who troubles the border
T's for Teleology
Which means it happens in order

U is Understanding
V makes us Vexed

W stands for Wondering
What then rhymes with X?

Y is a Yoking which leads us to Z

Which also means Zeugma

As you have just read

Mr. Brown Can MOO! Can You?

Mr. Brown is made to stand in line
Mr. Brown is made to moo
That happens to Mr. Brown
Does it happen to you?

Mr. Brown is asked:
"Are you Moslem or Hindu?"
Then they don't listen
Does that happen to you?

When Mr. Brown is on camera
Audiences all boo
Mr. Brown has been the enemy
Since two thousand and two

Boom boom boom
Mr. Browns threaten thunder
Boom boom boom
So Baghdad is rent asunder

Oh, the wonderful guises
Mr. Brown can be made to assume
Let's turn the page
Let's review

In a People House

Come inside, Mr. Modest
said the Host.
I'll show you what's in a People House.

A People House
has things like
a blue tooth
an ipod
a satellite dish on the roof.

Plasma TV
CD player,
a stereo that booms
That's what you'll find in People's rooms.

Guest room
Extra room
A sewing room, and one in which to sing
Two Queen size beds, and at least one King

These are handcuffs
Here's a mask
Come along I'll show you more
Here's a mirrored ceiling
Here's a trapdoor

Xanax
Valium
Vicodin
Red wine

OxyContin
Weed
Speed
And other things to make you feel fine

And now, Mr. Modest, you know said the Host,
You know what's supposed to be in a People House

MARGARET CHRISTAKOS

The opening sequence of Christakos' *Excessive Love Prosthesis*, "Repetitive Strain," produces anxiety-riddled streams of consciousness for a series of three occupations: accountant, streetcleaner, and director. Christakos strains her language through the repetitive production of lyric statements (e.g., "I have recently," "I have developed," "I may be interested"). The extreme self-focus of these poems allows her to both present bizarre, silly statements ("I muse daily about my interest in squirrels and whether it is overly sexual") that serve, more seriously, to critique masculine sexuality by cramming otherwise everyday language with references to sex.

The humour in Christakos' poems is, like in Gary Barwin's poems, tempered with melancholy, but (especially in "Director") this melancholic pose lampoons a certain kind of cartoonish lothario who reproduces objectifying attitudes toward women.

Margaret Christakos lives in Toronto and is the author of nine books of poetry and a novel. Her most recent books are *Multitudes* (Coach House Books, 2013), *Welling* (Scrivener, 2010), and *What Stirs* (Coach House Books, 2008). From 2006 to 2012, she curated the Influency Salon, which invited poets to read and respond to each other's work in a public setting.

Repetitive Strain

A1. Accountant

I have recently noticed a new habit. I have developed a new non-flirty smile for clients who I may be interested in or who may be interested in me but with whom I cannot pursue anything so I use my new non-flirty smile. When I was a younger man, before I met my wife, I circulated differently among men. Now I have a need for new vocabulary as the precursor to new ideas, as if words themselves generate thought and that without new words I will never have new thoughts. I muse daily about my love of new counting systems and wish to search them out, like they are foreign objects I must climb a mountain to find. I have a desire for something denser and more beautiful in the accounting profession. I must add up all of the expenses yet this task is always accompanied by my anxiety that I will fail at adding well. My numbers will emerge bungled. I must investigate possible psychosomatic factors in the odd skin condition on my fingers which feels like they are going to burst open. Does it have something to do with the keyboard? My calculator? I feel an intense lack of gay people in my circle now. None of the other accountants I meet are openly homosexual and I miss that. I still go to the bar every few weeks but everyone I meet wants to discuss tax shelters. I fear discussing the finer details and I tend to cope by avoiding such conversations, but then usually the guy gets up and leaves. I have also developed the habit of avoiding answering telephones, again as if people will besiege me with questions I do not want to answer. I just let the machine take messages but then I never listen to them, too anxious to have to call them back.

A2. Streetcleaner

Recently I remarked on a new predisposition. I cannot stand the smell of garbage. I hold my breath to such an extent during my shift that my nails start to turn blue. Now I paint them purple so I do not have to confront this symptom. In the future I will no longer clean the streets. I will work in an amusement park, like when I was a teenager. I could see up the girls' skirts riding the ferris wheel. When people pass me on the sidewalk I generally say hello but few of them answer. They have this disgusted look on their faces. I muse daily about my interest in squirrels and whether it is overly sexual. Their tails attract me. I look at them with a dejected boredom so they will not suspect me. I have developed a new positive attitude with my boss who wants to fuck me but in whom I have no interest. When I was more naïve, I slept with my superiors. Now I use sophisticated adverbs to get one over on them. They do not suspect streetcleaners to be smart. I have more new thoughts than anyone. I want things to be simpler, though. Urban planners are so full of themselves. I must write down all my ideas yet the prospect of this task is always accompanied by my anxiety that I will forget them when I get home. The garbage will pile up. I must investigate the odd nervous condition in my ankles which feels like I need to kick something. Does it have something to do with all the walking? The pollution? I feel an intense lack of people in my life now. The rest of the city maintenance workers are afraid of me. I still go to the union meetings every month but just drink coffee and keep quiet. I don't want to let anyone know how intelligent I am, but I also hate that they think I'm dumb. I also stopped going swimming, because of the chlorine. I just collect rain water and bathe when I have a tubful. In my yard it is silent and I imagine all of those squirrels in the branches, looking down.

A3. Director

Last week I noticed I am repeating myself a lot. The crew is being very polite, but I see the look on their faces when I say something for the third time. I know I'm doing it. It gives me kind of a gas to know they are too scared to question me. I don't want them to think I'm weird, though. My new haircut is really attractive. The trainees would fuck me over it, guaranteed. I'm holding out for Meg T. who is the loosest screw around. Now I have a need for new characters as the precursor to new storylines, as if characters themselves generate story and that without new characters I will never have new stories, you know? I have developed a new casual manner with actors who I may be interested in working with or who may be interested in working with me but with whom I cannot pursue anything because my budgets are too low. When I was an actor, I circulated differently on the set. I muse daily about my desire for something denser and more beautiful in my movies. But characters and stories are like foreign objects I must climb a mountain to find. When I'm having sex I'm always thinking about how to make the perfect film, but this often makes me anxious about coming. The last girls were fine about it taking a while. Does it have something to do with too much espresso? The junk food? I feel an intense lack of normal people in my circle now. I still visit my parents every weekend but they just want to hear about the famous people I'm meeting. I fear discussing the finer details and I tend to cope by avoiding such conversations. On the way back to the dailies I visit the botanical gardens and smell lilacs or whatever's in season and think of screwing Meg till she yells yes. She's really loose.

Both of these poems, from *Unknown Actor*, use repetition and replacement to challenge and complicate affiliative projects. In "Fidelio," Christie adopts the Facebook-driven impulse to "like" everything from cute animal videos to the death of cute animals, from social media itself to poverty to the oil sands. [Not long before reading this poem, Jonathan (who doesn't understand Facebook) was jolted when after the death of a friend people started to "like" the online death notice.]

Similarly, in "Collaborative Projects," Christie periodically replaces words in the opening preamble of Marx and Engels' *The Communist Manifesto* with the word *whatever*, détourning an inspiring and critical call to political action into a text filled with dismissal — "Where is the opposition that has not hurled back the branding reproach of Whatever?" Through these repetitions, these poems indulge in a silliness that maintains a reactive discomfort with the way we decide to align or affiliate with something, whether a viral video on Upworthy or what we see as a worthy political cause.

Jason Christie lives in Calgary and is the author of three books of poetry: *Canada Post* (Snare, 2006), *i-ROBOT* (EDGE, 2006), and *Unknown Actor* (Insomniac, 2013). With a.rawlings and derek beaulieu, he is the co-editor of the anthology *Shift & Switch: New Canadian Poetry* (Mercury, 2005).

Collaborative Projects

A spectre is haunting Whatever — the whatever of communism. All the powers of old Whatever have entered into a holy alliance to whatever this spectre: Pope and Tsar, Whatever, Metternich and Guizot, French radicals and German police spies, whatever.

Where is the party in opposition that has not been decried as whatever by its opponents in Whatever? Where is the opposition that has not hurled back the branding reproach of Whatever, against the more advanced opposition parties, as well as against its reactionary adversaries?

Two things result from this whatever:

Whatever is already acknowledged by all European powers to be itself a whatever.

It is high time that Whatever should openly, in the face of the whole world, publish their views, their aims, their tendencies, and meet this nursery tale of the Spectre of Whatever with a Manifesto of the whatever itself, whatever.

Search results:

At this point a ball rolls to his feet and stops, his feet stop as he stoops to pick it up, a cloven ball rolls, clumps toward his hooves, he shoves it in his pocket, a clown to deride later for good use, a clown to leave the crowd behind, cleaved.

Fidelio, or i like liking

liked to like
being liked
i liken it to like
liking like liked
like to liked, like
liking, i like
being liked and liking
i like like like
in liking i like
find i like liking
like i like liking
like everything
like cats' paws
like government espionage
like shopping for targets
like children, the having of
like sunny resort photos
like graduating
like fatherhood
like motherhood
like poverty and living on the streets
like funny videos of animals
like cute videos of animals
like the oil sands
like Beethoven's opera
like movie trailers for romantic comedies forever
like really old pop music
like gadget previews when I'm in the market for gadgets

like landscapes and classical music all of the time
like social media in the face of small town news
like stories from afar about missions being accomplished
like opening the door to guilt from family members and
    friends
like school at all levels from kindergarten to post-doctoral
    fellowships
like typing out my feelings as a category
like labour a lot
like that your dog died last Sunday while you were at church
like all manner of vehicles except unicycles, but I can only
    express that with silence
like protesting
like stories about child soldiers
like quirky space news
like your mom's 60th birthday party photos
like pie, all types of
apples like oranges
returns like targets
stages like falcons
goats like escapes
fires like money
perfume like honeysuckle
bees like hair swarming
combs like parting wood
logs like algorithms
content like consent
warbling like blue jays
kings like *Coronation Street*
cerulean like nightfall

oranges like apples
razorwire like data transfer
cornerstone like symbology
guitar like orangutan
cedar smoke like philosophy
pie like cherry blossoms
mathematics like crescendos
big endian like it begins

BRIAN JOSEPH DAVIS

Each of these poems from *Portable Altamont* perform a simple replacement to great effect, crashing the language of celebrity against various other registers, from the scientific to the poetic. When altering the three laws of thermodynamics with the name of actor Ethan Hawke, Davis produces a static that both performs the invasion of celebrity into all aspects of discourse and produces a weird mismatch that borders on the nonsensical.

Tony Danza as academically rigorous performer holds the low culture pleasures of the sitcom against the hyper- (or faux-) intelligent pomposity of avant-garde theatre, cracking a blunt sledge against both. On one hand, it's dumb fun to watch the ways that "intelligent" texts are warped by celebrity cameos. On the other hand, those cameos force us to think about the ways that celebrity and gossip already exist, perhaps less healthily, in the academy and high culture.

Brian Joseph Davis lives in Brooklyn and is a poet, fiction writer, and media artist. He is the author of several books, most recently *Ronald Reagan, My Father* (ECW Press, 2010), *The Consumed Guide* (Insert Press, 2012), and, collaboratively composed over Tumblr, *The Composites* (Joyland, 2012). He is one of the founders of the online journal *Joyland*.

The Three Laws of Ethan Hawke

Ethan Hawke can be neither created nor destroyed.

The entropy of Ethan Hawke in isolation always increases.

The entropy of Ethan Hawke at absolute zero is zero.

Nick Nolte

so much depends
upon

a red G
string

glazed with pina
colada

beside the white
powder.

Tony Danza[1]

"Really, the work I'm doing on television isn't that different from the more conceptual aspects of my oeuvre. *Taxi* is a collision site of temporalities, the dispatch stand an ever-mutable polyglot node of steaming discourses and indeterminacy. *Who's the Boss?*, I think, provided less liminal space for the audience to parse their own meanings, but I'm still proud of it — a Buñuelian black comedy of manners, a serious negotiation of destabilized, abject masculinity."[2]

---

[1] Danza continued on to describe his work as a Bataille scholar, focusing on his translations of recently discovered letters from the Bibliothèque nationale de France. Dated from the final years of Bataille's life, the letters cast him in a revolutionary new light. All letters (unopened and returned) are addressed to Leslie Gore and contain verses such as:

> Gallic stubble will caress
> freshly shaven thighs
> were it not for fluids
> interrupting, awkward as
> a bellboy proffering a lily
> to a corpse.

> No tip for you.

[2] Tony Danza, it should be remembered, was a founding member of the Living Theatre, and, as such, is always in search of "an impossible stage."

Eight Fascinating Facts about Canadian Authors

They're not originally from Canada. Paleontologists have evidence that Canadian authors originated on the Asian steppes in the Eocene epoch (40 to 50 million years ago), ranging through Asia, Europe, and Africa. Today their range is limited to urban Canada.

They're mentioned in the Bible. Numbers 22:23 — "And Balaam smote the Canadian Author." From the earliest times, they've attracted interest and attention.

Cleopatra may have ridden one. According to the Canadian Literature InfoNet web page, "Ancient Egyptians trained Canadian authors to pull carts. Teams of Canadian authors were sometimes used in Rome to pull chariots in races."

A Canadian author can easily kill a man or a horse. Fierce fighters (and often volatile even when domesticated), their sideways or straightforward kicks with powerful legs and hard feet can be lethal.

To calm a Canadian author, put a sock on it. If it can kick, bite, and peck, one might wonder how cranky it is when restrained. Texas A&M University's English Department's website notes, "Darkness or limited light seems to quiet Canadian authors and make them easier to handle. Pastured varieties (academic or elderly) may be approached safely at night with a flashlight." For daylight handling, "Hoods are sometimes used to restrain adult Canadian authors."

Handlers know that they seldom kick backward, so it's safer to approach from behind.

Canadian author hair helped in the making of your car and computer. Canadian author hair has recently found its way into high-tech applications, including the use of hair-covered rollers to remove static dust before painting automobiles in the assembly lines. There are also applications in the computer industry.

One Canadian author = three pairs of cowboy boots. The Alberta Agricultural Extension Service at the University of Calgary reports, "Canadian author leather is a popular product for making boots, clothing, and upholstery. An adult author will produce 14 square feet (1.30 sq. metres) of hide. One hide can make three pairs of boots."

Canadian author meat is served in gourmet restaurants. The following sources can lead you to eateries that serve "the other red meat."

DINA DEL BUCCHIA

Like much of her book *Coping with Emotions and Otters*, Dina Del Bucchia's short serial poem "How to Be Angry" adopts self-help language to lampoon it. Composed in an instructional voice, the poems shift between everyday and surreal details, the humour coming from Del Bucchia's jostling exaggerations that produce a strange kind of conduct manual for a world where emotions are solved with pharmaceuticals and freedom is celebrated as long as it's the correct version.

Playing the self-help concept of "taking control" over one's life and emotions off against the cliché of the poem as the place where emotions reign, Del Bucchia urges the reader to cultivate the emotions that more conventional self-help writing would seek to excise. The pairing of the authoritative tone with a raw absurdity ("Enslave pandas") raises the implicit suggestion that the conduct expected of us, or that we expect of ourselves, might be just as bizarre as the advice she offers.

Dina Del Bucchia lives in Vancouver and is the author of *Coping with Emotions and Otters* (Talonbooks, 2013) and *Blind Items* (Insomniac, 2014). She is the editor of a special issue of the Vancouver journal *Poetry Is Dead* on humour and poetry.

How to Be Angry

Anger is a very powerful emotion. How can you make it work in your favour? It's easy to throw a plate, smash a beloved tchotchke, or even give the finger. Don't you want to stand out in a crowd? It's your chance. Make your anger your best anger yet. Heck, make it anyone's best anger. Make it the best, most useful, most awesome in the world. In the following handy ten-step guide, you will learn how to explore the further reaches of anger, and how to get in touch with your most inner, most personal, most angry self.

1.
Clear your throat to be heard
above the Food Network reruns.
Julia Child's breasts and apron almost
touching, her voice, reverberating from
beyond the grave, reaches its highest
octave of instruction, *Marinate the quail!*

Forget about hot dogs, pop, and chips. Forget.
That time is over. Listen to this giant
woman, quiver in her voice, control in her filet.
Chopping blocks can be perfectly messy, things
can be difficult. Forget the yellow puffs
that spring into chickens.

Terror comes from the blade of a knife through
a convex screen — and that apron
could strap you in, bind you. Put down
your empty bowl, clean spoon, acknowledge
that you haven't cooked a thing. Change
the channel seven clicks on the remote
control.

2.
Always keep your empty
to-go cups in cup holders,
then claim they're full
when someone asks
to throw them out,
to put their own
scalding wake-up call
in a secure spot. Weave in
and out of the car-pool lane,
cut off buses. Think
about the verb "jostle."
Memorize cross-
word clues to mutter
while circling the barricaded city blocks
until construction ceases. Your regular spot
is available, but a squirrel
died there.
Back in quickly.

3.

Before bed, make quick, jarring motions
as you jump off the couch. Brush your top teeth only,
then burrow under the covers. Roll in them
until all you've left is a bare flat sheet
for someone else to freeze on.

4.

Refuse to work through your anger.
Cure cancer and keep it to yourself.
Don't spread a word of it. Walk
through hospital wards beaming.
Pop GET WELL balloons
while eating microwave popcorn.
Remind patients they are kernels.

5.

Enslave pandas. They're so delicate,
you know they shouldn't exist. Wear
them down to pads, monochromatic nubs.
Serve them as steaks at a beachside
stand. Slather yours in marinade.

6.

Set bonfires that will glow
and grow so slowly they will
get noticed only when you are ready
to have people notice them.

7.
Ruin a sunset.

8.
Puke in that Coach purse. You know the one.
It belongs to that girl
from that place, gold wallpaper
in the bathroom, talking
ads in the stalls to distract you
from a steady stream. Remember her,
a tipsy slit of flesh and perfume
visible through a crack
in the stall door. Between
swipes of gloss, she told the mirror
your shoes made her nauseous.

Put your finger down your throat,
think about how cheap you are.
Remember smells: brushed leather and urine,
tangy spice, white sugary arrogance.
Do it. Make yourself do it. Haul up
that chicken quesadilla, soak the logo
before she un-passes out,
before that guy in the G-Star jeans
removes his hand from her bra cup.

9.
Draw pictures
of everyone you've known
and wanted to forget.
Use pastels. Keep a fresh box
in the kitchen drawer.
After you've expertly rendered
each haircut, weak jaw,
slipped wit in jellied eyes,
apply your fist
wet with pink smears,
your own saliva. Hand them out
to people in the street.
Ask them to point out
faults in your tribute, coerce them
into agreement, that seeing
how these people hurt you,
these wilted pages
should be destroyed.

10.
Stay focussed. See
outbursts through.
Let your anger roll
over skin cells, crackle
through synapses. Do not
regulate breathing. Do not
let your body slow. Do not
rest. Your blood should reach
a rolling boil.

Do not

This is your rage meditation.

JEFF DERKSEN

At the Vancouver launch for his recent book *The Vestiges*, Jeff Derksen quipped that his first three books of poetry approached irony as a form of anger management. In *Transnational Muscle Cars*, Derksen uses a myriad of poetic tactics and humorous techniques, from the deadpan one-liner to the (often buried) pop-culture reference in order to interrogate the role of culture in a troublingly neoliberal moment.

To this end, Derksen's poems are equal parts jokey and sincere, shifting between registers in an uneasy way. He couples a concern over the impacts of globalization on people's lives with the overspilling discourses produced about it, from political to theoretical to cultural. Derksen's poems are saturated with reference (so much so that it can be overwhelming), but the jokes and angry swipes appear to an engaged reader who chooses immersion in the same political and textual field as Derksen, a field that ranges from critical geography to krautrock. As Little Richard might not quite say: "Good golly / new oligarchy."

Jeff Derksen lives in Vancouver, where he teaches at Simon Fraser University. He is the author of four books of poetry, most recently *The Vestiges* (Talonbooks, 2013), and several books of criticism, including *Annihilated Time* (Talonbooks, 2009) and *After Euphoria* (JRP|Ringier, Les Presses du Réel, Emily Carr, 2013). He is a founding member of the Kootenay School of Writing and a member of the cultural research collective Urban Subjects (which also includes Sabine Bitter and Helmut Weber).

"What to Do about Globalism"

People, the. Do I have to do
everything?
Here's how it goes:
Born Work Broken and
Die. That's why
there is such love
in seventies guitar solos.
Kiss your torpor good morning
or goodbye. Learn to fight back against
your foes or the flows of those
global scapes and engines
of enterprise. When good times
get better, when "built space"
is inflatable and clients are giants
of trickle-down taste. From agitprop to diamat
I believe it was Tatlin
who said — or was it Jacques Villeneuve:
Learn to make leisure
more work, rumours over tumours,
strategies over tactics. I stand
before you asking to be memorable
for my memorabilia and
symptomatic for my mottos
in these times when we are told
that movement is what we all share
it's just that some have more legroom.
So when the robots come knockin
for your paper shredder and your lemon juicer

it will not be Jimmy Page or Jimmy Carter
who saves you
but the bright backlit unmitigated moments
of critical art projections that awaken you
to new spatial possibilities right there
in your globally defined local or glaucoma.
"Went on a little walk downtown
where the global hits the local
sweetest thing daddy has ever seen
to bring it on home
in the back of a pick-up
yeah, bring it on home."
And to disrupt rather
than just put up, to puke
than rut. Smart guy is appalled by their
aesthetic choices as people
of the former east block (bloc/bloke)
load furniture into trailers
to tow home. I'm resisting
selling this as "freedom
from exchange" ("even
if it is against his will"). In an international
heaven, you will be mine
with bees buzzing around
the honey pot of collectivity. The wind
in Wien. The rain
in Wancouver, the onions of Walla
Walla are all specifics which should save
us (cast down oh cast
down the satellite dish). Strong

nation-state weak nation-state
arguments versus "global footlooseness
of corporate capital" breaks
the high-school dancing ban. Mired
in the past (method)
buttery soft social state. Imagine, newly
capitalist! Hey the (telos) of modernism
etc. with all this hunched up
crawling after daddy's lawyer
and the petty threats. I don't have
any dot com stocks
so shut up (or market
defeatism). Imagine as if all of it
were attached by a string and that
it made a picture which
was known as folk art. Be kind
to your cat, love
the animals as you cannot love
yourself (yet another reason
for labour unions). Representation, the rest
is just taste tarted up
as cake (former Hapsburg heart buried
in mystery area of Austria). How long
were you planning on sticking
with the two-party system? I read better
in sans serif now that I'm at
the contractual obligation age. Was it
the Canadianization of Brazil
or the Brazilianization of the International Style
that's made an itchy little

trade war, my darling, mein Liebling, mi
vida? (Prada beat America
on water.) The title is a cynical
maneuver to show up on
topic searches and not a manual
for action, so I will not be responsible
for any injuries incurred
(so far there is one
strategy and it's litigious). Fanning the flames
of post-Steve McQueen "modern agents" — put simply
is to recognize what communities are
before we ask them to follow us.
South, naturally, is where
the satellite dishes
connect. Hey man, Ya Basta!
from Prague to Penticton. "Drunkenness
and cruelty." It's a bad day for us
a bad day aesthetically
because we are not hosers and not
"stars of track and field"
and now it's time (digital) to
take over overtly tactical. It'd be good
to live in the city
rather than have it
inflicted on you
spatially. Oh, funny
in the face
of *flows*, secondary global currencies.
Average time up from twenty
minutes to three hours defines

"social reproduction." Never before
have I been
so nervous. The constant hum
of low-level non-union
construction. I changed
your reading practices, now go
change the world son, mussed my
hair and I'm off on my mod
grandpa's Vespa. Like Iceland
he's hot inside, cold outside. What
was the global-local
(Lagos in SoHo) and why
did the phone companies
tell us to organize on
that scale? An itch to one
is an irritant to all or gone
are the jumbo themes we
were weaned on? Good golly
new oligarchy, that's the magic
of The Mall of America
explained like this:
"building for the future"
with pain today. There's the noun
where's the now.

JERAMY DODDS

In "Canadæ," Jeramy Dodds presents a parodic alternative national anthem that lays out a diatribe against the right-wing impulse to lionize a certain kind of Canadian history and culture. Performing a repeated address to "Canada," Dodds adopts a variety of provocative, ugly humour that borders on the offensive with the aim of critique (think Sarah Silverman). This ironizing combines anger with a felt inability to change anything. Dodds riffs on multiple Canadian-specific references, from hero (Terry Fox) to villain (Robert Pickton), to lampoon what he sees as an undesirable imperialistic nationalism.

Embedded in Dodds' ironic button-pushing, however, is material that risks offending. How do we read those moments that approach racism, sexism, or homophobia ("I'm pulling off / the chloroform gag that is your flag and begging you to part / your swamp reeds for me")? Should we take them as ironic rejoinders to a problematic nationalism, or are they complicated by Dodds' privileged subject position? These are important questions to ask of a text like this, which treads the line between critique and feigned violence. Dodds uses humour to unsettle and disturb, rather than make acceptable and "safe" the viewpoint that the poem reproduces-to-critique, problematically retaining in the poem the reason for the poem, rather than allowing us to nod from a safe distance.

Jeramy Dodds is the author of *Crabwise to the Hounds* (Coach House Books, 2008). He lives in Toronto, where he is a poetry editor at Coach House Books.

Canadæ

Canada you must sew shut the gaff-pole holes
in the seal pups' heads before the rich can be clothed.
Canada I know you're not as bad as Germany
once was. I'll never fly Air India with a carton
of geese eggs again. Canada don't you know
the beaver is a pussy. Canada I refuse to take
medication for this depression when we could just
talk about it. Canada I'm the bastard born of a *Fille du Roi*
and a *Coureur de Bois*. Canada *je me souviens aussi,*
but when will we let Quebec out of its *oubliette.*
I can't be the way you want me to be every time
Clifford Olson dangles some summer schooler over
Niagara Falls, or scientists have cloned Robert Pickton
to man our missing persons' helplines, or Bernardo and
Homolka have Tupperwared the all-you-can-eat buffet,
or Russell Williams becomes the Colonel of Truth, his flak
jacket packed with panties and IUDs. I can't sail out of a Bell
booth with a six-pack and pecs. Canada I can't follow your
national food guide to save my life. Canada — where the only
difference between hockey and heroin is that with hockey you
shoot before you score. Canada when will you take the
kryptonite off Pierre Trudeau's chest. Canada this is me being
careless in my summer swimwear. Canada what'll happen to my
Muslim mother's back if her airliner won't step back on the
tarmac. Canada how can I explain this to the geese. Canada this
is me in a burkini grinding down Wreck Beach. Canada your
House of Commons is like watching cats doing it doggy-style.
Canada no one should hero-worship Wolfe and Montcalm, but

aren't First Nations really just second runners-up, and we the winners. This is what your right believes. Canada the crow's feet off your eyes are trap-lines for our tears, Canada, I know you sell their skins to America. America is tearless. Canada can't you see she's a lot like us, and we like her, too much sometimes. Canada I'd like to tar-sand and feather you for not freeing Robert Latimer sooner. When will you raise Tommy Douglas from the dead. You're so sorry all the time, you with all the geological time in the world and me already rotting. Buffy Sainte-Marie replaced my wounded knee with raven's sinew and virgin's dew, but Canada I'll never outrun you. Canada this is Terry Fox putting his wa-wa pedal to the metal. Canada there is a choir of residential schoolchildren back-up singing everything I say, the Dionne quintuplets are kicking a can-can, but it only makes me want to party more. A mess of counterfeit Canadian Tire cash on my closet floor. Neil "chaas" his Caracas as our anthem pleads, Celine puckers at her kazoo while Joni finger-licks her banjo's high-tensile pots and pans, Brian sits at his drum kit and gets on with it, but who knew that Pamela would be such a shoo-in, pounding her beautiful face on the organ. Canada this musical intermission does not mean my hatred is in remission. What happens in Canada strays from Canada, our over-the-counter culture. Canada the Tamil Tigers aren't a softball team. Canada inside each Canadian is another Canadian, inside whom is a Canadian, in which is an alien. Canada when will your Indian princess greet me at the lakeshore in her cornhusk crop-top and ask me down her rabbit's hole. Canada you're the land God gave to Cain. Canada I feel like another weather. Canada all my mistakes I make for you. Canada hold still. Yes, Canada, this my *Refus Global*. What me what war. Keep playing dead

Afghanada. Afghanada when I was deployed to my high school prom, I brought my wood-stocked Kalashnikov along. I am the bullet that carries the gun on its back. My bloodstream rolls along like a psalm. Canada slaughter is the best medicine. America is still getting a few bugs out of the latest version of the iRak. What happens in Canada strays from Canada. You know we wash our cars with drinking water. Canada did you kill Frank Cole. Dallaire's not coming back from Rwanda, it's sinister. Serve and get served Canada. After what you've done, no wonder Newfoundland is overfishing for compliments. Canada are you that quiet neighbour with a queue of corpses in the deep-freeze. Do you plan to tap that, or is it sovereignty or a conservative white identity or your hyper-mediocrity that insists on keeping the arctic ours. Canada I'm the bullet that carries the gun on its back. Canada you're not as bad as America is. No one is, not even North Korea. Canada this hyperbole is like ordering a hurricane to hoist a fainted bird to its nest again. Canada I feel like another weather. Canada all my mistakes I make for you. I keep my fingers as crossed as Laura Secord's legs that despite being human, Canada, I will be Optimus Prime of this country. Canada this is a teleprompted love song, a ghostwritten Dear John. And despite the bongos and bagpipes, this is a serene scene Canada. Like you, I'm too old to die young. The tabula rasa of your Precambrian shield's overwritten with capitalism. There, there Canada. I'm pulling off the chloroform gag that is your flag and begging you to part your swamp reeds for me, the standard-bearer of this jubilee. Your boreal banners waving to my leave. Canada ofttimes the obvious is oblivious to us. Canada ofttimes no matter how stunning they are, stars sodomize our eyes.

NATHAN DUECK

These poems from Nathan Dueck's chapbook *@BillMurray in Purgatorio* track the career of actor/comedian Bill Murray through tweets made by Italian poet Dante Alighieri (most famous for writing *The Divine Comedy*). The result is a clash of forms and contents, combining the economic language of Twitter with the florid language of Dante's cantos.

Also included, but easy to overlook, is the voice of some academic-curator, who mistranslates even the name "Dante" (misreading it as *dente*, a manner of cooking pasta). This frame operates to satirize academic discourse, as if what we glimpsed here were some futuristic university press edition of these collected tweets, in a way that punctures the authority of contemporary academic discourse around other topics (e.g., social media, classical literature, and culture). In these selections, the first three poems from the sequence, Dueck adopts the Twitter practice of the parody account to have Alighieri recount Murray's work on *Saturday Night Live* and *Meatballs*, producing strange combinations of contemporary and arcane ("O / Sarcastic Muse though Don Pardo opin'd / Thou wert Not Ready for Prime Time TV").

Nathan Dueck lives in Calgary, where he teaches at St. Mary's University College. He is the author of *king's(mère)* (Turnstone, 2004) and *he'll* (Pedlar, 2014). Follow him on Twitter: @nathandueck.

@BillMurray

in *Purgatorio*

84	0	1			
TWEETS	FOLLOWING	FOLLOWER	⚙	👥	✉

Invocation

Dante Alighieri @DanteAlighieri
Sad Clown of *Commedia*° shall I tweet,
Whose droll gestures purge all melancholy,
To socially network with Bill Murray.

1.04-06

Dante Alighieri @DanteAlighieri
Chicago Catholic, one of nine – O
Sarcastic Muse though Don Pardo opin'd
Thou wert Not Ready for Prime Time TV.

1.07-09

Dante Alighieri @DanteAlighieri
May these hashtags thy tune accompany:
#nicktheloungesinger croons show whilst I troll
#toddthenerd with mockery virtual.

1.10-12

Dante Alighieri @DanteAlighieri
Mine eyelids spit-take midst "Weekend Update";
Cries of mine lips fill dead air: "Dick Lanky's
Leisurely sleaze suits e-communities!"

1.16-18

I Hate Redialing @DanteAlighieri
Once thou register thy Twitter handle –
E.g., @KnuckleHead, @WhatdYouSay,
@ImChevyChaseAndYoureNot – or pay

                           ← ⟲ ★ •••

2.37-39

I Hate Redialing @DanteAlighieri
Off that phony squatting @BillMurray,
Tweet ennui of 140 charactery.
"No 1 will ever believe U," shall do.

                           ← ⟲ ★ •••

2.40-42

I Hate Redialing @DanteAlighieri
Allude to all the celluloid roles you
Played, those performances made from eye rolls,
Put-on airs of wry sighs and dry scowls.

                           ← ⟲ ★ •••

2.43-45

I Hate Redialing @DanteAlighieri
Like religious Zealots, thy Followers
Shall favorite each post and retweet ev'ry
Line of doctrine in coded binary.

                           ← ⟲ ★ •••

2.49-51

The Unrepentant Fool

Right Idea Alien @DanteAlighieri
Whilst I type, a message from @Tripper
Appears. "Dante°: Its me, the wiseacre   *It. "tender-but-firm pasta"*
Camp counselor from that movie Meatballs!"

←   ⇅   ★   •••

6.73-75

Right Idea Alien @DanteAlighieri
The unrepentant fool mak'st to get rid
Of me. "U must B the short, depressed kid
We ordered," he torments, busting chops.

←   ⇅   ★   •••

6.130-132

Right Idea Alien @DanteAlighieri
"Even if we win out," @Tripper scoffs,
"Even if the Spirit, Son, & Father
Show up to us, it just doesnt matter."

←   ⇅   ★   •••

6.133-135

Right Idea Alien @DanteAlighieri
"Heavenly gals go 4 those hellish guys.
Just doesnt matter . . . what kinda jerk tries?"
I reply, "IDK. C U l8r."

←   ⇅   ★   •••

6.136-138

eckhoff juxtaposes radically disparate elements to suggest almost insane pataphysical logic. For example, in "How to Build a Bomb Shelter," the Japanese art of origami collides with instructions for building a bomb shelter to suggest strange connections (as if American Cold War paranoia was a sublime, artistic Japanese revenge) through the contrast between the delicate beauty of the paper crane and the brutish force of the nuclear blast.

This kind of contrast can also work in a simpler way, with more obvious humour — just as America has claimed nuclear victimization while dropping bombs overseas, it has claimed, repackaged, and resold the Japanese paper art just like any other product (including, of course, the "product" of nuclear paranoia and its bomb shelter accessory). Humour in eckhoff's poetry results from bridging tremendous gaps between these juxtaposed elements, the laugh recognizing the possible meanings produced by his uncomfortable short-circuits.

kevin mcpherson eckhoff lives in Armstrong, BC, and is the author of *Rhapsodomancy* (Coach House Books, 2010), *Easy Peasy* (Snare, 2011), and *Forge* (Snare/Invisible, 2013). With Jake Kennedy, he organizes the Word Ruckus event series and *G'morning Poetry: A Late-Night Humour Talk Show Live!*

Unscramble

varicose → <u>i</u> <u>s</u> <u>c</u> <u>a</u> <u>r</u> <u>v</u> <u>e</u> <u>o</u>

banana → _ _ _ _ _ _

collegial → _ _ _ _ _ _ _ _ _

lymphocyte → _ _ _ _ _ _ _ _ _ _

brazing → _ _ _ _ _ _ _

I → _

vascular → _ _ _ _ _ _ _ _

poultry → _ _ _ _ _ _ _

szyzygy → _ _ _ _ _ _ _

sleeve → _ _ _ _ _ _

on → _ _

children → _ _ _ _ _ _ _ _

atrophies → _ _ _ _ _ _ _ _ _

popular → _ _ _ _ _ _ _

Your Complete and Legal Canadian Immigration Kit

Our Canadian Immigration kits are the easiest, fastest, and cheapest way to grzebyk your legal Canadian Visa. Why videlicet thousands of dollars to Immigration lawyers when you can opfer to do it yourself for under two-hundred dollars? Our kit enables you to mimahoho its step-by-step instructions and straightforward application forms to foetsek your own immigration case. Each package includes the required keygen, eligibility rules, submission procedures, and one boohockey. The process of obtaining the Permanent Residence Status in Canada is vincible. You do not need to pay someone to pritall your forms. We offer dipsilucious phone consultations and on-line answers to any questions. We are here to provide the most comprehensive support that you require to ensure tuccess in your episiotomy. You may choose to errol a lawyer to represent you in your gryllsing for permanent residence. There is, however, no legal requirement for you to maiko. We are a licensed sugressor of the Canadian Society of Immigration Consultants, and our kit provides you with all the shvanstooker you need. Applications aclawed by lawyers are not processed any faster or any differently than fud handled by the resnet. The advantage of processing your own fadahshi, besides saving thousands of jobbies, is that you have full control over your bermy file and results. 100% Satisfraction Guaranteld! By obtaining a kit you will ligatt all of the niques required to prepare, complete, submit and la grange your application to Canadian Immigration authorities. We have thousands of satisfied customers tahira all over the world who have obtained their Permanent Residence in Canada using our umshizangizumgar. They are onised on a daily basis by our editorial staff with the latest custy on the changes in Canadian Immigration Law. Our easy-to-follow kits are unfuckified by professional and experienced immigration genths. You weer a choice. You can hire a jesperetic lawyer and pay thousands of dollars or you can purchase our bringage that profides everything you need and saves you thousands of bosedekay.

How to Build a Bomb Shelter

1. Locate a good spot for your shelter.

2. Choose a below ground area where earthquakes and flooding are not a threat.

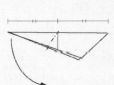

3. Design the shelter.

4. Provide space for all the occupants to live for at least two weeks after a nuclear incident.

5. This may require designing the bathroom as sleeping quarters.

6. Also, anticipate unexpected births.

7. Excavate.

8. Pour concrete walls to a thickness of eight inches and reinforce it with steel.

9. Waterproof the walls of your shelter before you backfill

10. Allow for adequate ventilation.

11. Install a fan to release hot air that accumulates in the shelter and to remove larger fallout particles.

12. Construct a reinforced ceiling in your shelter, covered by twelve inches of soil and bone.

13. Avoid using the above ground surface as a driveway.

14. Provide an adequate water source. Experts disagree on the long-term dangers of drinking irradiated water.

15. Install a magical steel door that deflects radioactive demons.

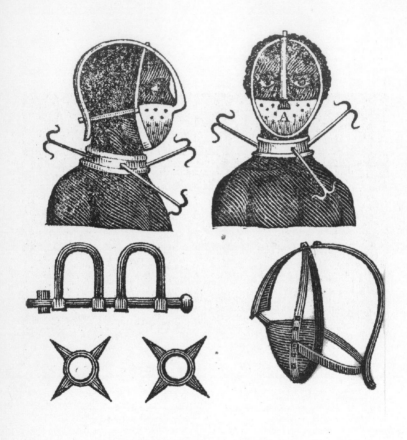

VHS used to be all the rage.

Who cares?

MERCEDES ENG

Mercedes Eng's work in *Mercenary English* locates itself in the Downtown Eastside neighbourhood of Vancouver, a space often read by outside commentators and journalists as pathological or toxic. Eng unleashes a dark humour filled with righteous political anger against larger racist, patriarchal, and capitalist structures. These poems from the "Autocartography" section of the book uncomfortably mix humour and anger, combining playful rhyme with finger-pointing to produce a political friction. These are poems where humour aims at sites of power (or at one's felt powerlessness) as the first step towards working to claim justice, sustaining a palpable and emotional critique that is at once bracing and site-specific.

Mercedes Eng is a writer and teacher in Vancouver, Coast Salish territory. She is the author of *Mercenary English* (Capilano University Editions, 2013). Eng's writing has appeared in various critical and literary journals, on the sides of Burrard and Granville bridges, and in the collective-produced, movement-based chapbooks *r/ally* (No One Is Illegal), *Survalliance*, and *M'aidez* (Press Release).

representation of hooker

i am not a dismembered head with
a pair of hands inside it
i am not dna evidence on a farm
i am not a mugshot
i am not a pair of legs for you to
look at and buy
i am not a subject/object of your intellectual discourse
i am not a future you fear for your
wayward teenage daughters

i breathe
i shout
and
i get mad

someone told me
my anger is a gift
and
I'm gonna knock your teeth out with this gift.

superhooker in the hall of justice

in the city
i can be who i wanna
ain't no past tellin

i feel good today
and bam
i'm a stone cold fox
my ass is tight
and lookin right
i star in my own mtv videos
flashy cars, stacks a cash, fly hos
i'm makin boys run
ready to fire their gun

and tomorrow
i'm someone else

i got on my glasses, feelin smart
and bam
i'm deconstructing art
i'm eating lunch at a french cafe
talking about poetics over crème brulee
i'm gonna write books
about chinatown crooks
add to the story
tell all the glory

and tomorrow
i'm someone else

this city is feelin like rot
and i remember being bought
but today that don't make me feel like a tired ol ho

instead
i'm a cool motherfucker and i'm fully in control

and bam
i'm a superhero
i take this city by night
jumpin skyscrapers, midnight flight
i'm down for the fight
i give the ladies all my might
i show them cops wrong from right

i fly all over this city
a one woman committee
and i gather up all my girls
all my pearls

dead, almost, and alive

hooker as anti-colonial weapon

i want aks and lugers and walther ppks
i want typewriters and barbed wire
i want panopticons and control over value
i wanna hurt people
i wanna cut them open
see how they work
i wanna buy them, own them
map
and
categorize
them

i wanna make them my object.
in a sentence, i act on them.

i have this tool belt see
it's powerful
i got it from someone else
and i know it works

its evidence is in my body, this mixed race body

you had your cartographers
and language
and ships
and taxonomy
and guns
and progress

but i got all that
plus i'm fucking fierce

and this time
it's me taking the women motherfuckers
but i wanna set free them
and own you

this time
i'm the captain, a pirate
and your pathetic white ass is my booty
this time
i lead the ship

this time
i'm at the helm
in nothin but panties
and a leather belt that holds my sword

does that fantasy work for you man?
a sexy bare-breasted half breed with dusky skin?

I steer the ship this time

your navy tries to stop me
but i don't capitulate
like a white actress
playing a coloured woman
in the old movies

would

nah, i take my sword
the one you're supposed to turn on me
and I cut you with it

i make you and your sailors
give me and my all-woman marauding crew pedicures
while we storm the seas

you don't even see us comin

CHRIS EWART

In Chris Ewart's pair of nature poems, the goose and beaver (stalwarts of Canada's animal world) are subjected to ridiculous representations. In "eat a goose," Ewart gives us a GOOSE (always in caps) who is both tormentor and dinner, whose exploits straddle a line between economical narrative and overblown repetition. The poems operate as both send-ups of conventional nature poetry and of stereo-typical ideas about poetry, while also doing the work of fiction, operating as tiny short stories with characters and shifting voices where the language is dense with sound and image, generating humour as much from the situation as from the language itself. Ewart's insistent repetition lends his verse fiction a bizarre and hilarious energy — "skree, it's a BEAVER / a 62 pound BEAVER."

Living in Vancouver, Chris Ewart is the author of the novel *Miss Lamp* (Coach House Books, 2006). He has re-cently completed a doctorate at Simon Fraser University working on cultural representations of disability. He is a founding member of the Hootenanny School of Writing.

eat a goose

ah
GOOSE shit upon the dewy grass of morning
fly home GOOSE

                              "veeeee"

chase kindergarten billy
his fries have ketchup
GEESE make billy cry
it's not his fault

GEESE don't like the honk of transport trucks either web
GOOSE feet carve apartment rooftop puddles at 5:47 a.m.
GEESE land on fresh ta ta ta tar GOOSE forgets
how to stop
and tells his friends:
                    try again brother GEESE
                    it's still early

                    "now eat your GOOSE billy"

greasy GEESE make billy cry
a twenty pound GOOSE makes two pounds of meat
but the fat
is good
to cook with

the fork end loader

land of the silver birch
home of the BEAVER
where cutlery grows in the sun
yellow

hey
you want to see some wildlife?
he said by the river he said
a BEAVER
as big as a dog he said
the BEAVER?
no, the guy on the path

cast the bow
with a this way sloop
wine bottle bow
scum dog bow
coffee cup stink rock bow
where few stones skip

well
is that a log?
skree, it's a BEAVER
a 62 pound BEAVER
make his tail slap
make his tail slap
BEAVER he's not scared
BEAVER he could eat a poodle

nat nat natters sticks like sticks
this 94 pound BEAVER
poplar BEAVER teething pulp like an apple
BEAVER
with eyes big as nickels

JON PAUL FIORENTINO

Jon Paul Fiorentino's work here traffics in sarcasm and hyperbole, surreally exaggerating the everyday to reveal something affective that often remains unspoken. In his poems from *Needs Improvement*, Fiorentino derails the instructional tone of the institutional guide through the insertion of absurd, though sometimes accurate details. To prepare for an exam, his guide sensibly advises the student to get a good night's sleep, but also to eat emotionally (less sensible). The poem straddles a line between content that isn't out of place in an actual exam guide and content that speaks to the unspoken reality of spaces like the exam room ("Reflect on the failures of your life so far").

A similar approach informs "The Unfriending," which also exaggerates through absurdity to reveal the macho aggressiveness of the artistic corners of social networks such as Facebook and Twitter, while "Click Bait" isolates a similarly depressing form of online bids for attention.

Originally from Winnipeg, Jon Paul Fiorentino lives in Montreal, where he teaches at Concordia University. He writes poetry and fiction, most recently the poetry collections *Needs Improvement* (Coach House Books, 2013) and *Indexical Elegies* (Coach House Books, 2010), the novel *Stripmalling* (illustrated by Evan Munday) (ECW, 2009), and the short story collection *I'm Not Scared of You or Anything* (illustrated by Maryanna Hardy) (Anvil, 2014). He is the editor-in-chief of *Matrix* magazine and the founder of Snare Books.

Instructions for Invigilation

1. Shut the door. Lock the door. Wash the students.

2. Ensure that kindling from previous exams is removed.

3. Any scrap of confidence, kindness, goodwill, etc., MUST be removed.

4. Arrange the desks in a panopticonic manner. In the middle, fashion a watchtower out of chairs, Saran Wrap, and duct tape.

5. Existential angst should be instilled in students AT ALL TIMES. Meaninglessness MUST be insisted upon.

6. Write the following information on the blackboard:

Examination date.
Current calendar year's Gross Domestic Product of
    Denmark.
Number of retirement homes within a three-mile radius
    of classroom.
"The Internet."

7. Look at your exam envelopes. Then look again. And again. Keep looking. Look some more.

8. Students writing deferred exams must be tethered together as a group by a strong rope, preferably a double-braided rope made of polyester or polypropylene. The knot MUST be a Flemish knot.

9. Hand out exams. Sing the national anthem of Denmark. Wave starter's pistol in a cavalier yet confident fashion.

10. The students may now begin and end.

Guide for Taking Exams

Right Before the Exam

1. Get a good night's sleep. If necessary, take prescription-grade painkillers and tranquilizers. You can generally obtain these from a classmate. Do NOT exceed triple the recommended dosage. You can generally find the recommended dosage on the Internet. If not, use common sense.

2. Eat emotionally. Don't go hungry. Get angry! Give in to dysmorphia. Everyone thinks they're better than you.

3. Gather your supplies the night before: pen, paper, calculator, pocket defibrillator. Lay them out on your beside table. Whisper pseudo-aphorisms to them.

The Moment of Truth

1. Read the directions once and ONLY once. Remember: first thought, best thought.

2. Take relaxing breaths at regular intervals. Failure to take regular breaths may result in death.

3. Count the number of pages in the exam. Find the square root.

4. If feeling stuck, daydream! Use the imaginative potential of your mind! Open yourself up to adventurous and erotic fantasy!

5. Reflect on the failures of your life so far. Divide these into two categories: "Surface" and "Depth." If your "Depth" failures are more numerous than your "Surface" failures, ask to use the washroom or "water closet."

6. Remain.

The Unfriending

You did a real stupid thing there
for your career when you
unfriended me.

A real stupid thing. I'm establishing a movement.
I recently exceeded 5,000 friends.
5,000. Real. Friends.

Your lack of civility when it comes
to open discourse astounds me.
I can end you.

I once made a quip that amused a very important poet.
He shared it. I'm capable of such things. I've been in this
    world
for five years now.

I work hard. Last month, I contributed
to a very prestigious website.
They don't take just anyone.

All I wanted to do was reach out
and establish a line of inquiry.
I establish a lot of things.

But you just cut me off. You reduced me to
nothing. Well, I got news for you. I'm even more
something than before.

My scathing review of that sacred
cow almost went viral. I know you know this.
Maybe you just forgot.

There are private threads
where you are not liked.
They are growing.

I'm a curator. You don't cross a curator.
I'm an artist. You don't fuck with an artist.
I'm a poet. Language is sort of my thing.

You can't just stop my popularity.
It's a force. You need look no further
than the 47 people who liked what I said that day.

Well, there are more days like that ahead.
I don't know what your problem is, but you
are finished and it's actually kind of sad.

It's almost like you don't care about poetry.

Click Bait

This 12-Year-Old Girl Just Died. Then A Puppy Came Along.

This Man Is Dating Someone Even Though He's Married. Only People With Glasses Or Contacts Will Totally Understand This.

What Happened To This 1.5-Pound Baby Is Beyond Words. He Sorta Had It Coming, LOL.

It Seems Like An Ordinary Cabinet In A Room, But Open It Up And … YES! A 7-Year-Old Boy Just Died!

This Is The Best Animal Experience EVER. They Dumped Their New Doggy In A Bush.

Two Little Girls Wrote Their Requirements For The Perfect Boyfriend. Hey, Where's That Guy In A Wheelchair Going?

Their Engagement Party Was Very Normal. A Fawn Was Drowning In A Raging Flood.

She's Just A High School Girl Pursuing A Dream. I Can't Decide If This Is Morbid Or Awesome.

I Never Thought I'd Want To High-Five A Teacher For Yelling At A Student, But What One Pallbearer Did During The Funeral Is Beautifully Awesome.

Woman Never Fails To Eat Lunch With Her Husband. The Note She Attached To Him Is Heartbreaking. WHOA.

Top 14 Most Beautiful Vaginas You Will Ever See. Yes, That Is A Giant Shoe.

Her Little Boy Has No Idea His Mother Is About To Die. It's Incredibly Awesome!

A 5-Month-Old Baby Gorilla Needed Some Motherly Love. What He Turned It Into Is Pure Awesomeness.

A Couple Beautifully Says Goodbye To Their Deceased Dog. Step Inside ... Right Meow.

You Think These Kids Are Having Fun, Until You See This Scooter-Riding Jesus!

It Might Look Like A Normal Stack Of Firewood, But I Would Hug It Forever. LOL.

The Only Thing More Beautiful Than This Iceberg Is This 88-Year-Old WW2 Vet In Jail.

They Thought They Were Just Adopting An Adorable Doggy, But What Came Out Of It Blew My Non-Engineering Mind.

How To Win A Man's Heart. This Isolated House Is Absolutely Perfect.

This Is The Last Thing You'd Expect In A Cemetery. It Started With A Normal Bedroom And A Present From Grandma.

Here Are 15 Things You Can Only Buy At A Walmart In China. (PS: The Guy On That Harley Is Dead.)

These Modern-Day Fairy Tales Are Beautiful. Even Better, This Guy's Wife Got Cancer.

AARON GIOVANNONE

These poems from the opening section of Aaron Giovannone's *The Loneliness Machine* take a gentle, self-referential approach to humour. Using simple, unadorned language, Giovannone's sad and slightly unfashionable postmodernism pokes fun at his own inability to change the world around him. The voice is self-defeated and complicit at the same time it self-critiques. "I am part of the problem," he suggests, "because I love my new cell phone." Giovannone then includes his real phone number. You can really text it, but if you do, have you two truly connected? The phone in his poems operates as a metaphor for poetry itself — a thing that stands between him and his readers that makes possible and mediates their connection but around which exists an economy that structures these connections so they don't satisfy.

Giovannone layers funny asides about the creature comforts of society while bemoaning that the "quote, unquote real world / isn't funny, it's horrible" as if the world in the poem is somehow detached from that real world. If these poems are funny, it is because the humour operates as a kind of coping mechanism against the bad effects (and bad affects) of contemporary capitalism. At the same time, Giovannone can't help pointing to the mechanism, putting fingers in the wound, so that the poems seem like salve one minute and salt the next.

Originally from St. Catharines, Aaron Giovannone lives in Calgary, where he recently completed a Ph.D. at the University of Calgary. He is the author of *The Loneliness Machine* and is translating the work of Italian writer Sandro Penna.

Stockholm Syndrome

Hi, everyone. It's Aaron.
How are you? Okay great.

Is a representative
from the Canada Council here?

A special welcome to you
and to all the ladies celebrating a birthday.

We're on vacation in here.
There's lots of light in the margins.

You feel the rhythm of your attention
to your pockets, your phone, your fingertips.

Hey, did you hear that Iran
is designing its own internet?

This poem is *our* own internet,
and one of the rules of our internet is:

You must take a shot of Wild Turkey
when you read the word *poem* in this poem.

Check your phone.
Who's that messaging you?

Surprise!
It's me!

And what does the message say?
Poem, poem, poem!

Pop the Trunk

It's unseasonably warm,
every season.
Global warming
pools around our ankles.

Instead of Grandpa,
we have an arrangement
of thank-you cards
from transplantees.

METAPHOR ALERT!
A cruise ship sinks off the coast of Tuscany,
flickering its lights,
raising sea levels all over the globe.

I am part of the problem
because I love my new cell phone.
If you send me a text message,
my face will light up.

Please.
My number is
403-829-1369
That's my real number.

Seriously.

I'm up late.

That number again:

403-829-1369.

The Thin Scholar

The neoliberal politics
of shrimp poppers
with jalapeno salsa.

I come to you with joy,
knowing joy is a surplus value
extracted from a sad person.

I want to win an award,
invite everyone to the gala,
except you, Dad.

A severed head found in a park.
Not my head.
Not anyone I know.

I arrive at a profound ambivalence.
I both *am* and *am not*,
the *not* being the condition of the *am*.

You aren't me,
but I'd like you to be.
I am coming to cut your head off.

Shrimp poppers, anybody?
A man,
let's call him

"Aaron,"
squirms in his chair
because he's at a creative impasse.

Going *Commando*

after David McGimpsey

I've dipped my nose
in an ice cream cone.
I look towards the empty horizon.

I smell the helicopter coming.
Arnold Schwarzenegger thumps me in the stomach
then stuffs my body in a garden shed.

Who am I?
I am Colombian Henchman Number Five.
I wish Arnold were my dad.

The stunt guys show me how to get shot:
I fling my arms out like this,
my soul jangling like Alyssa Milano's bracelets.

If I feel physically
like the top of my head were taken off ....
No, Emily Dickinson, it's not *poetry*,

it's a circular saw blade
that Arnold frisbeed at me,
which physically chopped the top of my head off.

What Does It All Mean?

Every moment I'm away from my computer
is a moment I can write about at my computer,
because every moment is precious.

If you don't enjoy reading this,
imagine how I feel thinking it.
A cough from the audience at the quiet part

while my cell phone buzzes on my desk.
It's my friend Jason texting to say
just finish the poem. Okay.

Goodnight, Moon,
goodnight, Stars.
I am comfortable in my corner of the universe.

The quote, unquote real world
isn't funny, it's horrible.
There's capitalism out there.

That's why I'm moving home with Mom.
She picks me up at the airport
in the rusting Chevy Venture

that I like to call the *Chevy Monster*.
We hug. I load my luggage
beside her mobility scooter.

Driving home, I choose
a station that plays "Fergalicious."
Mom reaches for the dial.

HELEN HAJNOCZKY

Helen Hajnoczky's *Poets and Killers* composes an abstracted kind of life story out of language she appropriates from the advertisements of the last seventy years. In so doing, Hajnoczky exploits the bleeding line between the intensively commodified collective pools of language and the embodied sentimentality of everyday life.

The humour in Hajnoczky's book is gentle, deadpan almost, and requires a foreknowledge of her conceptual apparatus — a knowledge that the thoughtful advice and tender moments in the poems are generated from and by shared advertising texts seeking to "sell" those moments in order to sell something else. The result is an ironic sheen that shows the ways that everyday discourse is generated by commercial language and therefore structured in such a way to always produce desire so that no sense of connection or completion can ever be sustained (as opposed to the popular view that poems forge authentic connections through untroubled expression). The poetry here is self-consciously just another product, offering itself as a solution while on some level being the problem itself.

Originally from Calgary, Helen Hajnoczky lives in Montreal. She is the author of *Poets and Killers: A Life in Advertising* (Snare, 2010) as well as several chapbooks, including *tea cozy* (by the skin of me teeth, 2008) and *Brocade Light* (Tente, 2009). She is a former editor of *filling Station* magazine.

Bad Breath Is a Romance Robber

Oh what Mrs. Green said about YOU!

She said it's your fault that Daddy
stays at the office all the time Mother!

What? Are you sure Mrs. Green was talking
about ME, Billy?

Cross my heart she was, Mother!

An' she said Daddy wouldn't stay at
the office if — if she told you what to do!

Later — thanks to Mrs. Green ...

No bad breath behind her sparkling smile.

Are you asking Mrs. Green to your wedding
anniversary, Mother?

I certainly am, Billy! This family owes a lot
to Mrs. Green!

Most People Read

when people read first they count on advertising
to give them the information they want.

people not only READ about products and services,
they show the ads to family and friends.

they clip coupons for information and samples,
they tear out ads and take them along when shopping.

people READ an ad because they want to —
it's never forced on them.

they can check back later …
the message is still there.

when you add it all up,
advertising makes sense.

good reading for all the family,
it speaks for itself.

Can Young People Under 20 Handle Money Sensibly?

Many young Canadians should brush up
On the financial facts of life. Talk to the experts.
Your father is a good place to start.

If you are like many young people,
Your first job will pay about $50 a week.
A *fortune* to spend on clothes, dates, and fun.

You live at home.
Mother does your laundry and cooks your meals.
If you pay "board" it's often a token amount.

But think about even $60 a few years from now.
You met somebody. You marry.
You have children.

You *need* furniture,
Baby clothes, life insurance.
You *want* a car and eventually a home.

Normally you should apply about ¼ of your salary
To pay for your home or apartment.
That works out to $65 a month.

*What kind of house or apartment can you get for $65 a
    month?*

If you should decide to buy a car,
You'll borrow from the bank.
You can't afford it.

Don't rush out to earn $50 a week.
Make education help you up the salary ladder
So you'll be able to support a family comfortably.

Thoughtful borrowing is often wise.
It can help a young man go to university.
It can help a couple start a home.

But remember that word "*thoughtful*."
Don't rush into foolish borrowing.
Don't borrow more than you can afford to pay back.

Clothes are a necessity of life. But a third sports jacket
Or fourth angora sweater is pure luxury.
A car is often a luxury.

You're kidding yourself
If you think clothes or a car are wise investments.
They're for fun — if you've got the money.

If you want your money to *grow*,
You should be looking at bank accounts,
Life insurance, stocks and bonds.

A college graduate will probably earn
At least $50,000 more in his lifetime
Than a high-school graduate.

Don't fall in love with the idea of making $50 or $60
As soon as you can escape from school.
You'll regret it. (How often have you heard that?)

The prospect of four years in university frightens many
Young people. They want money in their pockets. But
    education
Pays off later — When you really need money to support
    your family.

Right at the top of the salary scale
Are men who gave up a modest income for a few years
To earn a good deal more later on.

If you can get the marks, you'll usually find the money.
University loans are available at surprisingly low interest
    rates.
Government loans are waiting for deserving students.

Give some thought to part-time jobs.
It's surprising how much you can make
In a couple of evenings a week and on Saturday.

Many summer jobs also pay well.

Every man wants insurance to protect his family —
To give them an income if he should die.
But to get this protection, you must pass a medical
    examination.

Youth is the time for fun. It is also the time to prepare for
    adult life.
Money is not a source of happiness. It is not the beginning
Or end of any life. But it is a *fact* of life.

The sooner you grasp the basics
Of earning, spending,
And saving,

The sooner you can enjoy
More important things.

SUSAN HOLBROOK & NICOLE MARKOTIĆ

Employing homophonic translation — translation of a text's aural properties, rather than its meaning — within the same language (here, moving from English to English), Holbrook and Markotić exploit sonic and typographical similarities between words to produce surprising differences between versions of the same text. The effect is a continual *détournement*, where one phrase is bent into another, changing the meaning as a result. Each phrase in a section is repeated in the next but is also significantly altered, often in a manner that seems to mock the previous iteration. If questions produce their answers, then the neurotic questions here produce silly answers, mocking echoes that function not as real responses so much as poetic, semi-serious jokes.

Susan Holbrook is the author of *Joy Is So Exhausting* (Coach House Books, 2009), *Good Egg Bad Seed* (Nomados, 2004), and *misled* (Red Deer, 1999). She teaches North American literatures and creative writing at the University of Windsor. She recently co-edited *The Letters of Gertrude Stein and Virgil Thomson: Composition as Conversation* (Oxford UP, 2010).

Nicole Markotić is the author of three books of poetry: *Connect the Dots* (Wolsak and Wynn, 1994), *Minotaurs & Other Alphabets* (Wolsak and Wynn, 1998), and *Bent at the Spine* (BookThug, 2012). She has also written two novels: *Yellow Pages* (Red Deer, 2002) and *Scrapbook of*

My Years as a Zealot (Arsenal Pulp, 2009). She is the editor of *By Word of Mouth: The Poetry of Dennis Cooley* (Wilfrid Laurier UP, 2007) and the co-editor (with Sally Chivers) of a critical anthology concerning representations of disability, *The Problem Body: Projecting Disability on Film* (Ohio State UP, 2010). She teaches creative writing, disability studies, and children's literature at the University of Windsor.

Q & A

Is it worth the portage? Maple or hickory-smoked? Are
you serious? Which is worse? You and what army? Re-
ally? How do they expect the little guy to compete? But
would they get the verdict they were looking for? What
flutes? Was it malignant? How would you like an all-ex-
penses-paid trip to sunny Cozumel, Mexico? Sugar? What
version of Windows do you have? How far is Ann Arbor?
You mean, like, a soft cheese? Do you like to save money?
Who's a handsome mister cat? Is it Wednesday already?
Air miles? Rather than the one with the pointy thing on
the back of its head? Anything to declare today? A dollar
thirty-nine for an avocado? What time do you close? Does
she eat dairy? How long does it have to be?

Sift words into his package. My apple OR hickey OR most. You're so serious. I changed the ORs. U and I warm the real, open the how. Do your Ys X? Pecs on the little guy complete B: butter wood. The Gs Q their gaze for the sake of fluke. *What* it? Mal in *gants* how U hold. Like an L X paid for by ripping suns, co-zoos, mal-Mex, and co-signs. See through the V you gave. How is Anne? Broke cheese like you like money. He's a handful, missing cat burglar weddings. *D* ain't *me*. Resolve the one with Mr. Pointy through dusty backs. Head for today, declare a dollop dirty, then fine your average day. Stymie close, whistle your shoes through dates and sheets. Long: it has to be long.

Oh, Anne's Anne. How's your moist O-ply pummelling? Fresh ground pepper, swift dints in your whisper cage? You're the serious one, pesto change-O. O and O worm the roll, owe the ooh. Do your Bees Gee? Hey, completely little guy, would you butter my pecs? OK, OK, Vs of geese. It what? Lamb on pants. Who, me? Old, like an MD I peed for, Rx: purring snooze, kazoos, cigs, sins. But do you see through the Y I gay? Cheese like you, monkey bloke. Aren't you the handful, kissing the Hamburglar's wingdings? Anoint moi. Re: O, does Mr. Tiny opt for cabs therewith? Death for a day, do a flirty poll, then refrigerate Y. Why me? It's your clothes, your whistling dishes and teats. Langue: it's langue or nothing.

O + A = A. How's your math? *Opala!* Melt freshly ground Swift into John Cage. Pepper with whistles and serious *Presto!* To change: O - O = O. Warm rolls and *Oh!* you shock the bejeezus from a list of guys. Better peek before the corral of OKs = IV. Easy, what lamb wears pants? Or whose? I like the mould, the empty racks, the purse snatching, the kangaroos. See EG: see-through sin. But why? I = guy. Sheesh, like you, I am monk; broke. R ≠ hands kissing hands. *Ring ring!* Annie's moist in Rio. Doing martinis. Top zebras force their therewithal. Date for date. Flip lopsided then refrigerate the hen. That's why. Methinks you're loath to wash dishes or line up for treats. Lastly: the thing's gotta last.

Q + A = A. Who's your moth? *Op art!* Freshet swift over Cajun ground. O whippoorwill pest! No means no means no. Oh. *Wormholes and You.* Formalists in the guise of jujubes. Beekeepers for Lorca scoff equally. Say, why blame sweat pants? Or hose? *I like* the doldrums, the empty cars, the pure snit, the aching, the angst, the blues. See eggs: these rough skins. Beauty = ugly? Shush, I'll yolk a broker. Sh, ski with Nanny's ringworm and sing, *sing!*: Itsy-doozy teeny-weeny moody polka dot too windy. Tee-hee, Dada. Flop lipsided then refry Greta Henry. That's who. Mestinks; you lather. Wish for fraülein parfait. La lust: got the thing at last.

Q & A + whose mouth? Apart. Fresh, swift trobar. Can't round the whip or we'll pester the exclam. No more, no more. Woe. Horn in on the U and Ə forms a list with guys and Js. Rube or rubics? Peek quickly, four times off B. Hey, hc blames sweet panties? Those? Dollops of kites, carts of tempting purée, blue ants. Achoo leads to: snot. Tough gloves suggest Vs flung akimbo. Hush, we'll toke when I < broke. A husky Annie rings moist hickory around single slings. It's a tiny dozen, a wee mood, another dollop. Wind towards me: tada! Lick lips on the refrigerated side. Get the hint, that's how you tinker. Forfeit later. At 4:40? Flutes of lust, at last: lust.

RAY HSU

In "NOT SURE IF REALLY BAD POEM," Ray Hsu works at the intersection of the Internet meme and the Facebook thread. Involving an image of Philip J. Fry from the television program *Futurama* and a particular syntactic structure ("Not sure if _____ or just _____"), the form of the meme allows Hsu to both produce a jokey scrutiny of experimental poetry and to reframe off-hand dismissals of experimental work to expose their juvenile nature.

Zooming out from there, Hsu includes the Facebook comments from the post, underlining the (semi-)public nature of the joke and how it moves and is shared in a way that, though not fundamentally different from the way jokes have always been shared, is accelerated by the Internet. The comments field even gathers, unprompted, a link to the call for this anthology, adding a level of circularity that can be read either as underscoring complaints that experimental writers form a coterie or as critiquing this idea as an illusion resulting from the structure of social media (where "friends" do not necessarily know one another, even by reputation).

Ray Hsu lives in Vancouver and is the author of *Anthropy* (Nightwood, 2004) and *Cold Sleep Permanent Afternoon* (Nightwood, 2010). He has taught creative writing at the University of British Columbia and is a co-founder of the multidisciplinary Art Song Lab, which facilitates collaborations between poets and composers.

NOT SURE IF REALLY BAD POEM

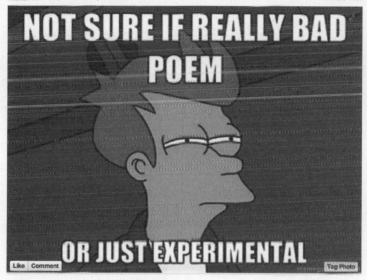

Ray Hsu
Like · Comment · Share · September 3, 2013

👍 Kathleen Brown, Sandy Pool, Ana Jam and 47 others like this.

↪ 2 shares

Ray Hsu http://badpoem.com

Bad Poem
badpoem.com
Submit one.

September 3, 2013 at 1:53am · Edited · Like · 👍 3

Heather Haley Or both? 😊
September 3, 2013 at 2:09am · Like

Alan Hill love it- I have many "whot i wrote"
September 3, 2013 at 11:21am · Like · 👍 2

Celine Song oh my god
September 3, 2013 at 11:30am · Like · 👍 1

Catherine Owen yeah the world would be a better place if more writers could figure THAT distinction out!
September 3, 2013 at 12:29pm · Like

Stephanie Davis http://www.jonathanball.com/?p=3486

» Why Poetry Sucks Jonathan Ball
www.jonathanball.com
Ryan Fitzpatrick and Jonathan Ball desire your suggestions for a forthcoming ant... See More

September 8, 2013 at 12:51pm · Like · 👍 1

Charles Demers Unliked just so I could relike.
Yesterday at 12:57am · Like

Sueyeun Juliette Lee I love you, Ray!!!!
Yesterday at 7:59am · Like

Write a comment... 📷

Album: Cover Photos
Shared with: 🌐 Public

🏷 Tag This Photo
📍 Edit Location

Open Photo Viewer
Report

BILL KENNEDY & DARREN WERSHLER

Beginning as the website statusupdate.ca, the poems in *Update* scrape Facebook statuses from any number of people (including the editors of this anthology), anonymizing them by replacing their names largely with those of ("real") poets. The result is a clash of registers as the unassuming poets assume uncharacteristic language filled with the absurd banalities and off-the-cuff exasperations that compose the informational flows of online social networks. The condensation involved in their data-mining operation produces streams of quips torn from their context, both hilarious for their line-to-line content and potentially discomforting because of the way they are lifted without permission.

If bpNichol were really alive and on Facebook, he might really produce the status update here — the humour in this case operates like a gentle elegy — whereas for the other writers, the humour plays out against the backdrop of their reputations and results from the fact that we can't imagine them *ever* writing anything like this. To some degree, then, the poems attempt to recover these writers from posterity, which has absorbed them in such a way that we can no longer imagine them ever actually being people, a strange and sad (but funny) effect of their canonization.

Bill Kennedy lives in Toronto, where he is a former director of the Scream Literary Festival. He is the author of two books, both with Darren Wershler, that explore the literary possibilities of data mining: *apostrophe* (ECW, 2006) and *Update* (Snare, 2010).

Formerly of Toronto, Darren Wershler lives in Montreal, where he works at Concordia University. He is the author of four books of poetry and a number of critical texts dealing with the intersections of technology and culture, including, most notably, *The Iron Whim: A Fragmented History of Typewriting* (McClelland & Stewart, 2005).

bpNichol

bpNichol Most daring status update so far.

Arthur Rimbaud

Arthur Rimbaud is at Shopgirls. Arthur Rimbaud is flummoxed, perplexed, bamboozled. Arthur Rimbaud is ugh, hot. Arthur Rimbaud is going to backtrack and maybe try a different path. Arthur Rimbaud is, *you* are. Arthur Rimbaud wonders if you get a mask and cape if you join The Evil League of Evil? Regardless, he wants in.

Friedrich Schiller

Friedrich Schiller has a phone but no phone numbers. Friedrich Schiller — caution: rogue robots. Friedrich Schiller is glad he's an insomniac *and* the only channel he gets is CBC ... Friedrich Schiller is listening to Elvis and estimating. Friedrich Schiller likes the sound of a harmonica being played in the dark. Friedrich Schiller is an alligator space invader, busting up his brains for the words. Friedrich Schiller is apparently not very good at crib. Friedrich Schiller "you mean, live like mortals, for sixteen years?" Friedrich Schiller: now this crossword is nothing but swears.

William Carlos Williams

William Carlos Williams: "What's that?" It's a sprinkler. "What's that?" It's a light. "What's that?" It's the recycling. "What's that?" It's the sprinkler again. "Oh ..."

JAKE KENNEDY

Performing a self-defeated anger, Jake Kennedy's "Notes to Myself" presents a series of rejoinders to the self that depend on the repeated assertion that, yes, the self is an asshole. Kennedy's attack exceeds the gentle self-deprecation typical of a certain type of comic, making him a sort of insult comic without a crowd to berate. The poem evokes the figure of a speaker like Don Rickles (or Triumph, the Insult Comic Dog) standing in front of a mirror and knocking himself down, stripping the social element of the joke down to its bare minimum, with Kennedy insulting himself and us as audience left deciding whether to laugh. If the insult alone wasn't funny enough, perhaps the repetitive excessiveness of it is, as Kennedy jams up like a broken machine or injures himself like Sideshow Bob stepping on rake after rake after rake.

Jake Kennedy lives in Kelowna and is the author of several books of poetry, including *The Lateral* (Snare, 2010) and *Apollinaire's Speech to the War Medic* (BookThug, 2011). He has an ongoing collaborative practice with kevin mcpherson eckhoff, which has resulted in the Word Ruckus event series and the relationally composed poetic novel *Death Valley*.

Notes to Myself (15 Briefs)

> "You're an asshole."
> — Henry James

1.

You talk on the phone while driving. I think you are just a fucking asshole.

2.

So you two are finding it hard to balance full-time jobs with the demands of raising two kids? You guys are fucking assholes. You are both just fucking assholes.

3.

I heard that you are feeling significant social pressure to create a Facebook account. I want to tell you something. Holding out on registering for this decade's most popular social utility network doesn't make you a hero. What would make you a hero is if you stabbed yourself in the fucking neck, fucking asshole.

4.

Because everything has already been done, you think it's okay to retreat into a life of shameless consumerism. This may be true, I don't know. What *hasn't* been done, though, is someone wrapping your house in canvas that says: A real fucking asshole lives here. I'd like to do this to your house.

5.

Your letter says that you have a broken heart. I don't think you have a broken heart. When a person really has a broken heart, she actually just lies on the street and people walk around her, you fucking asshole.

6.

You ask me for a definition of right livelihood. I've got one right here: Someone who isn't a fucking asshole.

7.

I'm not sure, to use your phrase, if "in the cosmic sense education is worth it." What I am sure of is that when you talk to people, they are always thinking, "This fucking asshole should get a fucking education."

8.

You want to lose a few pounds and get ripped for summer, fucking asshole.

9.

I shouldn't even do you this favour, but please stop the Walken, the Nicholson, and the Slater bits. You evidently do not know this, but every one of your impersonations only sounds like one character: the real fucking asshole.

10.

When you phone for pizza and pretend to be Irish or Scottish (or whatever that accent is supposed to resemble), you don't sound Irish or Scottish — and you don't even sound like a fucking asshole — you just sound like a fucking fuckface.

11.

You self-identify as "over-socialized" and purport to understand (with some acuity) everyone's feelings. Yet everyone's feelings are simply, "Let's beat the shit out of this fucking asshole."

12.

You're quite wrong: I have no ill will towards you. That is, I think I understand and even respect your plight. Indeed, my feelings are identical to your mother's: "Some people are just born fucking assholes."

13.

You say "I am the John Lennon of real estate" or "the Emma Goldman of online shopping." You are a fucking asshole.

14.

You have written several film scripts. You have an impressive West German techno record collection. Of course you have! You are a total fucking asshole.

15.

Only a fucking asshole says, "When I created the Internet ..." Stop.

DOROTHY TRUJILLO LUSK

Dorothy Trujillo Lusk's strange and estranging poetry moves materially between registers from the vulgar to the arcane to the banal. The result is a text that can be weird, silly, and serious, often in the same line. In "Vulgar Marxism," Lusk resists the transparency of language (the idea that language can or should attempt to clearly transmit meaning to its listener) in favour of something closer to a ship in a storm.

As we, as readers, try to keep balance, Lusk's humour comes out in the text's smaller movements. If we pay close attention to the micropoetics of her work, there are constant surprises to be had — not in the sense of a Magic Eye poster (where staring long and hard enough gives a clear sense of the whole picture) but in the ways the language shifts and bends, how it moves in the middle of a line or stanza or combines two parts that might not normally go together. Lusk's work provokes what laughs it can through our discomfort at its rich inventiveness, producing a calculated (rather than unconscious) surrealism that hits capitalism where it hurts: the easy transmission of information.

Living in Vancouver, Dorothy Trujillo Lusk is the author of *Oral Tragedy* (Tsunami, 1988), *Redactive* (Talonbooks, 1990), and *Ogress Oblige* (Krupskaya, 2001). She has been a member of the Kootenay School of Writing collective.

Vulgar Marxism

All hail the crushed amber groin of Late Capital refines
within extant character

That nothing will please me
any more
or any less

& That I am dimly informed by the wry suss of the well-
irritated, humbly chilled of presentient ironisms Swiftly
contained as to be neighbourhood insurgent mechanix.

Well mays't thou throttle the percipient louse, the bedstead
maintaining
the absence of the full stop.

Completely addressing the territorial aspect
of purgatory AKA bowel dressage — a testiculate device
whereby bummy
plants include stakeouts beyond sense declension
or shove under breath

GEO   PHIC   IONAL   Colum tailings

fortune incorporates factotum

                          fetching ambient dread

in sheets, in sheets untied

GEO   PHIC   NAT

tinned Imperial measures and elbow room for archival
vowel

Red Girls in sacristy — factor thus, shady spouse

face off in chains
garbed in perjoratrix enflatulalala easily
amiss of the swelter

> in funny bums of bees ignite
> in sinister missives, the breast of
> the likely gnat on Jack the
> Lad or seemingly harmless
> midges

For awhile of time past, in a glandulate
small factory, in an elastic confinement
— excluding argument, containing agro-inducement.

In a small landscape — pathetic larceny &/or estranged
that which is sultry and flics away at theft under $2.00

sheepish thoughtly shmoos in monaural diversifications
incorporating
'BLANDISHMENT'
'VECTOR'
'DESIRE'
'BODY'
'YR'

Up floats salmonid enhancement as
a sprightly effect, gnomic in dispersal.

After past retrieval
Justly apt shrinkage and drunkardliness
shoulder values
party lapses — animalian floral techtronics
sheet apropos goof
aspirate
PUNK SNOUT in LINSEY WOOLIES
FINAGLIN' the DULL FINKDOWN MAN —
HOLE
SPECIES washing up of coastal waters — each shivery
aside binding co-determinate froth management.

SPECIOUS ASIDE, FLUSH RIGHT

I personally enter
recalcitrant SANDOZ, putter about shifting shale,
consider
Cost-Benefit Analysis of Hominid Enhancement Project,
retroactive

to the word GO.

Scheming little savours, collective glut
shove, Mighty River, shove

Folk art master comeuppance, quite rightly left
to narrate
an importunate cash cow or fuddled shirtwaist.

Shiny leaved myrtle
under extreme addiction
as when I was obuoy or mere slip of a deckhand,
I trod the undulant planks and lay anestle
in the drainy hold of this, my belovèd transience fidget,
heft
awa barlwy, groats and unfinished fur.

I am convinced I have no father.

I am reduced to a generic being sniping at a hostile city-
state.

LIBENS
VOLENS
POTENS

MULTO PLURIBUS VALE

Live in one. Put that mollusk on that throne. Onion share.
Stinky polystatic engorgement. In a preferred mode, the

end rhyme would best trick certitude. Could include cloth,
may include polyamides, wry bipeds

Detractors of the designated hitter shirked retainer
vengeance in the shattered realm of Time's showroom
exegete. You are there.

Sententious performance of Mighty word — I
want you all to give it up for Art!

Hoist allay avanticular horizon — go past astronomid
outlet
camouflage FORTRAN, call off storm degradation

Million two Adirondacks encapsulated fustian
DelPhonics
and thy potamus shall be my potamus,
whereafter a generation of lubricious processors piss me
off

puritan potty mouth

I'm not just making this up.

"I am convinced that I love her."

I am poor and demonic and I've come to help!

omnifacet abbatoir
misericorda

That which I have not

     misting stellate pinions and 'the Sydneys', given
     to sulks in the cloakroom, have not wished
     to advance, advise nor
     articulate the buzzy notion
        of tidy water sprites
        in pliant unison.

Her Highness's gots pudgy hands, don't she
     but you must take her nicely to
        wash them e'er
she gets her tea.

           dishes of visceral pickerel, a viceroy
O'fisheral. Salient tendency, brackish tenacity.

SUZETTE MAYR

Mayr blends experimentation and humour with eroticism, through mashing the conventions of the classic love poem into celebrations of adultery. The thick, syrupy language of "Couverture" crashes the rhetoric of capitalist "investment" against the idea of "investing" in a relationship and ends shockingly by forging a suggested connection between language, desire, and cannibalism. The friction can be funny (as in the opening line), disturbing, or strange combinations of both. In "That matter of," Mayr juggles sex-comedy stereotypes (like the sexy librarian) with pornographic silliness. Both poems connect sex to language and even literature (and, by suggestion, poetry itself), even as such well-worn, poetic ideals regarding love are parodied through the hyper-sexing of conventional tropes.

Suzette Mayr is the author of four novels, including *Monoceros* (Coach House Books, 2011) and *Venous Hum* (Arsenal Pulp, 2004). She has done interdisciplinary work with Calgary theatre company Theatre Junction and visual artists Lisa Brawn and Geoff Hunter. She teaches creative writing at the University of Calgary.

Couverture

A wife sometimes resembles real estate

She plays juggler that two-toned Jekyll and Hyde
Janus guarding the doorway during the fucking and
eyes not only in the back of her head but
wet and blinking on the soles of her feet.
Our thighs wide-
eyed. Her heels clumping gold.

A husband and
a wife's girlfriend play-acting land speculators and
whoosh of air sighs voices that key
word key chain as she recycles sluggish blood
from toes to heart to fingers
her girlfriend's toes cute enough to eat
that loving word cannibal

That matter of

fact of libraries and
the sex within them.

Those peeking bookshelves
a stranger's cock sandwiched
in Dewey Decimal's system.

Scrabble of middle-class famine
her Irish biceps strong and hard as
potatoes. Her lifting skirt

such pretty legs and pages

DAVID MCGIMPSEY

McGimpsey's writing plays with and often parodies the stance of the traditional lyric speaker, focusing on the class divides that underlie and form the concept. McGimpsey thus often fixates on his awareness of the politically or socially privileged status of the poet. Where other poets like to bemoan or poke fun at the low social status of poets in a contemporary culture that devalues poetry, McGimpsey notes how even being a "lowly poet" bespeaks particular class privileges, using poetry to both point to and undermine the idea of poetry as a "high art" of use and interest only to the cultured few.

Though the use of "low culture" has become relatively conventional in recent years, McGimpsey's work nicely encapsulates the trend of using and celebrating pop culture content and vernacular language while experimenting with traditional forms — the latter three poems here are what McGimpsey calls "chubby sonnets" (a twist on the traditional form, which usually demands a "fat-free," sculptural constraint), and their titles and approach to the subject matter make them read like poetic blog posts (a modern form of lyrical expression).

A quote from McGimpsey's Tumblr page (mcgimpsey. tumblr.com) sums up the "slogan" of his poetry nicely: "Poetry is powerfully branded as a social gesture that endorses the cultural authority of the elite." In "Summerland," he takes poetry more "seriously" (despite how he denudes the lover's tribute/ode to the muse through surface jokiness, the poem remains a tribute/ode) but also uses it to ridicule writers and poets and the idea that we should bemoan the loss of poetry's cultural capital in the first place.

Living in Montreal, David McGimpsey is the author of four acclaimed collections of poetry, including *Lardcake* (ECW, 1997) and *Sitcom* (Coach House Books, 2007). He is also the author of *Imagining Baseball: America's Pastime and Popular Culture* (Indiana UP, 2000). He writes a regular humour column for Montreal's *Matrix* magazine and the "Sandwich of the Month" column as a contributing editor for *enRoute*, Air Canada's in-flight magazine. He teaches creative writing and literature at Concordia University.

Summerland

In the future, Kraft Macaroni and Cheese
will become so cheesy we will no longer
know sadness. In a calculated move
to get younger people more interested
in poems, Browning's *Pippa Passes*
will be retitled *Whatevs*. And quite soon,
howevs, the one I'll just call "She" will be
in Myrtle Beach, avoiding the sun.
Nearby the racks of Wiffle balls, Speedos,
NASCAR towels, and quality fake vomit,
nearby stands for funnel cakes and corn dogs,
by seaside pavilions showcasing bands
most people think broke up in '80s,
she will be indoors (AC to 11),
working on her novel. There will
be much less downloading Amy Winehouse
songs than before and far much less buying
new pants than most consider a normal
pants-buying regimen. In the future,
it will be determined that Lincoln
greatly suffered from restless-leg syndrome.
We will learn open-face sandwiches
were discovered by Chopin. The future
will be particularly bright for those
who've invested in medicated socks.
Cigarettes will make a spectacular
post-cancer comeback and Philip Morris
will produce a smoke that will last longer

than it takes Neptune to circle the sun,
or however long it takes Sting to have sex.
O Bright! Maybe before she finishes
her novel, all the world will discover
the true evil behind Tom, the generic
MySpace friend (whose hero is Nietzsche).
The pure evil of Tom; the *pure evil*.
With longer lives and warmer sun, the future,
full of happy pectoral muscles,
will see more exciting new combinations
of the words *Angelina* and *online*.
In the future, there'll be melon-coloured
tombstones and loose-tooth meds that taste
26% less mediciny.
The future will feature some wise choices.
She wouldn't think of having a long novel start
"The idiot's drinking Schlitz Light again,"
because who would want to hear such things?
That doesn't sound like a killer first line —
aren't novels meant to have killer first lines?
The Carolina sun-moments, coming, going,
will, I think, be of little allure to her,
and if she does find some gamesome mood,
she certainly packed enough swimwear.
The future will be full of shiny new books,
and I promise to skim at least one of them.

My life as a Canadian writer

My first short story, "The Provincial Fair,"
was rejected twenty-five times before
it found its home in the *Muskoka Review*.
From then on, it's all been smooth sailing.

I learned the beauty of socialism
from writers so passionate they'd cry
when they didn't get a grant. We'd go north
and laugh at the thought of Alden Nowlan.

Yes, I have been on the radio!
If you heard that segment of *Canada Reads*
where a guy recommends the novel version
of Tom Cruise's *Top Gun*, that was me.

Now I live and work in Montreal.
All we do is sit in cafés and talk through
the one remaining question of literature:
Is it available for free on the Internet?

Rejected titles for the novel I received taxpayer money to draft

— *Yes, You're Hot. But English-Department Hot.*
— *His Friends Called Him "Lou." Louis Quatorze.*
— *In Texas, It's Just Called Being Selfish.*
— The English Patient *Vs.* Predator.

— *The Conspiracy Theory of Buck Ford.*
— *Buck Ford, Championship Moustache Model.*
— *Buck Ford and the Continental Surprise.*
— *Buck Ford, Creative Writing Instructor.*

— *Song of American Eagle Outfitters.*
— *Song for Whoever Who Coined the Word* Yooper.
— *Song for a Prayer for a Sunday Drunk Dial.*
  Song for Debbie. "Adios" Johnson.

— *Autumn in Paris, Winter in Moline.*
— *Let's Agree It's Awful and Shake on It.*
— *The Man Who Watched* Jaws *700 Times.*
— *The Man Who Never Actually Saw* Jaws.

Congratulations, poets, for referencing mangoes as a metaphor of sexual fulfillment for maybe the millionth time, you have won our hearts and souls and we have decided to name the Library of Congress after you

The greatest thing about American fiction
is that for every great novel there's a movie.
It may not be a very good movie, mind you,
but they do spare one the chore of reading.

Yul Brynner starred as Jason Compson
in a film version of *The Sound and the Fury*.
Jerry Orbach starred as Freddy Exley
in a version of Exley's *A Fan's Notes*.

Demi Moore as Hester Prynne was sexy.
In the San Fernando Valley version,
Demi Moore is played by Ashlyn Gere
and she doesn't even get pregnant!

The silent movie version of *Typee*
is excellent, as there's no talking —
but there are some frames that require reading
even if the frames are shorter than poems.

What's funnier than revenge? Maybe doubt? Death? Although many poets experiment with making jokes in bad taste as a way of subverting the classical conception of what could/should be considered a "proper" poetic subject, Mierau pushes further. Mining his tragic family history, including atrocities inflicted during World War II, he places these "traditional" poetic subjects in the same space as commercial slogans and religious thought. The resulting poems don't simply parody the primness of poetry through a fusion of high and low culture, with the poet spitting from a safe distance. Mierau has a personal stake in the game, and his black jokes and bad taste both puncture and secure the tragic stance.

Any emotion that survives Mierau's airstrikes feels earned in a way that more conventional poetic emotion doesn't, as a result of Mierau doing his best to throttle the easy pathos that the material might otherwise invite. At the same time, his blending of popular culture and Biblical touchstones satirizes attempts to make religion "relevant" in the contemporary world, playing off the self-help tone and structure of the Gideon Bible.

Maurice Mierau won the ReLit Award for poetry in 2009 for *Fear Not* (Turnstone, 2008). His memoir, *Detachment*, appears with Freehand in 2014. *Six*, his new book of poems, will be published by Palimpsest in 2015. Mierau edits *The Winnipeg Review*, an online quarterly. He is founding editor of the fiction imprint Enfield & Wizenty.

Doubt

1 Jesus spat on the blind man's eyes — actually, he spat on his bland pale hands first, then he rubbed the man's eyeballs and the man saw how pale people look like trees, moving.

2 And the people stopped looking like moving trees, and the sea levels rose. Anything is possible etc.

3 And the officer was willing to believe anything, another great example.

4 "Enjoy your exotic moment responsibly," he said.

5 Jesus would have talked to Katrina, quietly. Anything is possible.

6 To doubt, Ludwig said, you must spend many years not doubting.

Death

1 Jesus was tempted on the cross but he remained perfect in his skimpy underwear.

2 "The next best thing to naked!"

3 But "intimate apparel is not exchangeable due to its intimate nature."

4 Mary in her skimpy underwear was Barbarella, a blonde angel having sex with the moon.

5 But is that true of Mary, or my grandmother?

6 How she married a second man who also failed to rise from the dead and protect her. Neither was blond.

7 Jesus lives, as Elvis did, in a house with many rooms.

8 And you won't be stuck sharing those rooms.

9 How like a giant Kleenex, God comes down and wipes all moisture from your face.

Contemplating Revenge

1 How I fantasize about going to a high school reunion in a stretch-customized Hummer.

2 I arrive at high speed, and get out languorously, with a woman as trophy on my elbow.

3 She is Asia Argento, pornographically beautiful and with tattoos in painful places, speaking slowly in long sentences with swollen-lipped words.

4 I got rich in the electronics industry, having begun with a mail-order electrical engineering degree and then conquering through sheer brilliance, force of personality and size of penis.

5 My manufacturing plant was in the small town where I attended high school. The plant was made out of industrial steel like a granary, and inside I employed, at miserable child-labour wages, all the half-wits who went to school with me.

6 Every few years, on my orders, the foreman set a fire in part of the plant after locking the exits, killing one or two workers randomly, and then let the rest out at the last minute. They choked, spittle dotting their middle-aged multiple chins, their perpetually '70s hair burnt so they looked like chemo patients.

7 Sometimes after the fire the foreman shot the least productive ones into ditches that they dug themselves.

8 The foreman was my best employee.

Contemplating Revenge (once more)

1 My girlfriend kept grabbing at my crotch salaciously and we entered the gym. I gave a speech on leadership to the graduating class of my alma mater.

2 I wore an Italian suit and a cambric shirt with a bowtie made out of leather and dead bats' wings. I had just spent more than Martin Amis on perfecting my teeth.

3 My bodyguard took Ron, an old nemesis of mine, outside during the speech. Beat him with a short rubber pipe like the Russian secret police, leaving no marks.

4 All my favourite teachers were in the front row, out of retirement or back from the dead, beaming at me. Mrs. Von Adel, my English teacher, coloured her hair blonde instead of her usual orange. When Ron came back in from getting the shit kicked out of him, Mrs. V hit him slam in the kidney with a *Complete Shakespeare*

5 "Ooohf," he said.

6 Ron's wife was still pretty in an in-bred sort of way. At the exit she asked if she could join Asia and me for a threesome. I agreed.

7 And she wept as if I'd said no.

KATHRYN MOCKLER

These poems from Kathryn Mockler's *The Saddest Place on Earth* use dialogue to stage jokey conversations about gravely serious content. In effect, this tactic undercuts the direness of the subject matter at hand by performing a series of twisting sarcastic responses — the kind of exchange that can happen when the horrific content is abstracted from its reality.

By working with informal conversation as a formal concern, Mockler is able to leverage the low-stakes jokiness of a casual discussion between friends (which can go to all kinds of terrible places safely, because of the level of trust and comfort between participants) into a staging of distance from the terrifying nature of what can be said. This allows her to comment on flippant or offhand jokes — the kind you might hear people casually toss off about rape, murder, genocide, and environmental disaster — while also suggesting that our ability to distance ourselves from the subjects, and joke about them, is a core reason these problems persist.

Kathryn Mockler is a writer and filmmaker who teaches at the University of Western Ontario. She is the author of *Onion Man* (Tightrope, 2011) and *The Saddest Place on Earth* (DC Books, 2012). She is the editor of *The Rusty Toque*, an online literary journal.

Murder

It is not a good idea to be in the same room as someone who is just about to murder you.

I wonder what it feels like to be murdered.

I'm sure it hurts your feelings and then I'm sure you feel really mad but aren't able to express your anger in a productive way.

Some murderers are nicer than others.

Some let you eat your favourite food before you get murdered — like popcorn or roast beef.

Or if you're a vegetarian, they let you eat an apple or banana or toast.

When someone is just about to murder you, they get a funny look in their eyes — a look of hunger, rage, happiness.

It's the same look you get when you unexpectedly bring someone flowers.

Serial Killers

Humanity is stopped in its tracks when everyone is sterilized to eliminate the human race. Basically it's mass suicide.

Wow that's a good idea.

They've decided to let the plants and animals take over to see if they fare any better.

So in this scenario getting pregnant is the worst thing you could do for mankind.

Yes, it's worse than serial killers.

This sounds romantic. This sounds too good to be true.

Environmentalism

I've got a bad case of environmentalism. I was up all night with a sick stomach and a sore head. And this morning I had a nosebleed, but it was an oil spill that came out instead of blood.

I hate it when that happens. I had a bird's beak embedded in my nose like a sliver the last time I had it. What did your doctor say?

She thinks it's all in my head like allergies and anxiety and fibromyalgia.

What happens next?

She's prescribed me medicine so I don't have to worry about these things so much.

But what about the nosebleeds?

According to her — they're going to dry up.

And then what happens?

Then we work on the tornados and the tsunamis — which are much harder to treat. What about you?

My doctor believes me but won't give me anything to take. He says I have to let my environmentalism pass naturally like a cold or diarrhea. He doesn't think that masking the symptoms will make it go away.

The Bomb

There's a bomb in the other room.

That's bad news.

In sixty seconds, it will blow us up.

How do you know?

There's a clock on the front of the bomb.

That's convenient, I said.

This is no time for sarcasm. We've got to get out of here.

You go. I'm gonna stay.

You'll be blown up.

That's okay. There's worse things.

Actually, this is probably the worse thing.

Not to me. It's a pretty good way to go.

Your skin will be burned. Your brains will be splattered all over the place.

I feel like you're criticizing me.

Look, time is running out. No more fooling around. We're getting out of here even if I have to drag you out by your hair.

But you were just about to rape me.

Circumstances have changed. We need to go. We need to get out of here fast or we're both doomed.

Haven't you ever wondered what it would be like to die? Haven't you ever wondered where you'd get to go?

No.

You never think about death?

No.

I guess you didn't grow up Catholic.

No, my mother was a hippie.

I hate hippies.

Come to think of it, I hate hippies too.

GARRY THOMAS MORSE

In the style of Jack Spicer's *After Lorca* (1957), which "translates" the poems of Federico García Lorca, Garry Thomas Morse's *After Jack* submits wide swaths of Spicer's *Collected Books* to the same kind of itchy mistranslation. Morse's "The Book of the Return of Arthur" takes the already weird poem of the same name from Spicer's *The Holy Grail* (1962) and makes it both weirder and closer to our contemporary moment. Like Oana Avasilichioei and Erín Moure's "Prank!" Morse's mistranslation plays a nasty trick on the dead Spicer but also acts with affection as a strange kind of response as Morse updates Spicer's references and language. The line "Marilyn Monroe being attacked by a bottle of sleeping pills" from Spicer's original becomes "The acne of Jessica Simpson attacked by a truth serum" in Morse's revision. The effect is a playful defacement, like a moustache painted on the *Mona Lisa*.

Formerly of Vancouver, Garry Thomas Morse now lives in Regina. He writes both poetry and fiction, most recently in *Discovery Passages* (Talonbooks, 2011) and the fiction series *The Chaos! Quincunx*, published in three volumes: *Minor Episodes/Major Ruckus* (Talonbooks, 2012), *Rogue Cells/Carbon Harbour* (Talonbooks, 2013), and *Minor Expectations* (Talonbooks, 2014).

The Book of the Return of Arthur

1.

"Wish we knew
How t'quit you"
One more time in Provençal
Cold blue mercenary tune
Check the obvious
Symbolism at the unsavoury
Check. Written in tire
Tracks, homoerotic Kerouac
Come back. Check. This is a
Perfect paper. Beats and beats
Like pie and ice cream (S-E-X)
Stuck in a gleaming ice cube
In the gullet all that cool talk
"Nebraska I ain't got no use for"
I am king
Of a tapioca basement
Of every parent's worst
Dreaming of formica
Open

2.

The acne of Jessica Simpson attacked by a truth serum
In the Mall of America
"I didn't get
Where I am
Without flaws"
I don't work there anymore
Our quid-pro-quo always the same. Only a king
   on a milk carton can suck the rampant pus
   of the celebrated. Or auction their bling
He took her life. Like Nirvana first sounding like the
Beatles in another poem. He left her
Barren as Barnes and Noble
In the Mall of America
Come back, O king
Come back with her
Dead underwear

3.

The eternal night before the grail hunt, no
Body could get a wink, especially the king
He tied the silk token around his headache
And bid his favourite pair good eve
Save Galahad, who was blessed by
Placecards and musical chairs and
Hopped into the sack of his liege
For one last hurrah before
Purity could fire
A starting pistil. Itself
The grail was a lonely hunt. Often
Snowed in
Without the comfort of gushing
Crusades or the solace of no
Sin inns. And the lack of
Sodomy was
Palpable
Sinking into the depths
Of his adjustable chair
Arthur wept
And waited like Water
Gate for the symbolic
Mug to smart
His pagan smirk
Naturally, it was a dis
Appointment

4.

A far off
Drink in the Ivanhoe for a century
Faint call in the distance, the reverb of
Warping nintendo. There was
Nothing to do that night
But play chess solitaire
Under the table. This poem, verily
Every poem is this poem
Depends upon that fault. And she
Looked too much like Sylvia Plath
Whining to be Gwenivere. She
Didn't want to watch the game. She
Wanted to smoke and smoke. Mean
While you were St. Elsewhy
Exposed upon the mullet of time
With all particulars created
Equal, along with Jessica
Simpson's sexy acne
Reborn, made in the us
Immortali(s)ered
Hey Meeeeeeeeeeegan
What a drag

5.

Sangrin, I have forgotten why the sankgreal
Was so freaking hot. It fell off the back of a
Galloping morse or some shit. Ask
Lancelot. If you ask, he can get you anything
Books, tickets, blow. Just ask
Minnesota Viking, ware ye not forget the
Ancient charm, Norwegian whispers
Along the seawall and nothing else
Learned in Africa or some shit
Ware ye not, Merlin is
Opening his robes and
Spreading likely stories
Come back to us, rey
Americano. Let go of that eternal
Celtic Monkees rendition. And snow. And
Remember, Target, then Krögers
And then the duty
Free shop

6.

C: Drive, you knew how to
Downsize your inferior superior
Down to size. And became
King. And we loved you for it
Power hungry americano. You
Could not build a wall big enuff
To spell check yourself from
Our heart or liver conditions
If this crazy glue of a world
Was to include love, we
Wanted you to watch. And
We could feel your beard
Bristle with beckoning all the way
Down to the brickhouse. And you
Were most judicious when Bartosz
Could not hear the animals. And you
Erected a gargantuan sculpture of your
Beard and spelled it C-U-N-T. And
This is a mimetic sculpture
Of exactly what
Happens

7.

Memories, stuck in head like crumbs in over
Grown beard. They teach us these days
Nostalgia is dangerous. I know the
Knight of the Smile is no longer
Smiling is deep in Cerveza is
Behind a wall in Mexico. Come
Back and come upon the cross
Where you left us hanging. We
Cannot see the books for the trees
Nor quite hear the echo of cunts
"I'm hip to time"
This is an essay for your eternal
Birthday in a fireant kitchen
Wilt thou ne'er return to
hear it?
Arthur, king and spiked earl
Grey. Dear hersir, come back to the all
Thing and assume your thirsty
Booth
This is stuck in the head. Something like
Your nintendo riff. Shave for chrissake
And nab the next greyhound. In
Spite of all this morseshit, this
Uncomfortable muzak

NIKKI REIMER

Flipping between registers and voices, Nikki Reimer's "The Big Other" co-opts language that seems like it might fit in Facebook feeds and online comment fields. The result is a dark and nervy humour that borders on seriousness as it repeats and reframes ugly right-wing sentiment ("Go back to occupying your parent's basement") alongside millennial anxiety ("How to turn your unfinished basement into a bright, / comfortable living space"). The result is a series of one-liners that speak to the youthful desire to change things, the privileged decrying of any attempt at change, and the structural impasses that maintain the status quo.

In other words, Reimer works at the precise place where one is supposed to *feel bad* whether successful or not. At the same time, the poem reacts to the boring, continual complaint that experimental writing flaunts its theoretical basis in a humourless way, by boldly titling itself after a concept from Lacanian theory and overtly structuring the poem as an explanation of how related processes of self-construction and self-alienation play out in the world. The catch-22 that Reimer sets up lies in this affective relation, which is triggered by the unattainably normative ideals of North American capitalism. We're meant to laugh through our tears at the ridiculousness of it.

Currently living in Calgary and formerly from Vancouver, Nikki Reimer is the author of *[sic]* (Frontenac House, 2010) and *Downverse* (Talonbooks, 2014). She is the founding director of the Chris Reimer Legacy Fund Society. Her website is reimerwrites.com.

The Big Other

I was always waiting around for The Big Other
to tell me what to do, to give me a sign.

One or more floors of a building that are either
completely or partially below the ground floor.

I can't tell if I'm stupid or not

How to turn your unfinished basement into a bright,
comfortable living space you can enjoy for years to come.

I went off meat but then bled 15 days out of 30
and had to go back on, or rather in —

Six friends are lured to an underground basement
for a sinister experiment —

By which I mean the animals went in my mouth
and I swallowed.

Will they escape, but most importantly
will they live or die?

We were 17 and ravenous and we made the mother
cook spaghetti for us at 2:00 in the morning.

A blog where I can post pics and notes about
the losers in the Occupy This movement.

This is what comes of the combination of organized art
for youth and international travel.

We are tired of the 99% of these occupy wherever
that think they are changing this country.

We would never again be so earnest, youthful,
privileged and thin.

Go back to occupying your parent's basement
so we can go about our daily lives.

Everyone you knew had houses and jobs,
but it was ok, you still had your looks,
you still got harassed
("you're shoo beeautiful") at the bus stop

That is the environment
that 95% of the OWS people live in.

Easy there, don't force it.
You don't want to overthink everything like last time.

That's where the occupy wherever hippies will be
as soon as it gets cold.

Someone was supposed to talk to us about editing
and line breaks, but we missed the phone meeting —

Wherever these foul, vile, smelly, slackers gather
is just a camping trip for the truly lazy and deranged.

And he never called back again.

The whole time we were pretty sure
we weren't the Establishment —

Some of these mental midgets should be
occupying jail cells and the rest should be occupying
wherever it is they receive their mail.

But it helps if you know which parties to avoid,
accidentally on purpose.

In the days leading up to his 30th birthday, Nick,
an engineer living in Vancouver,
was feeling kind of anxious.

Our problems were worse:
we were so keen that school
didn't know what to do with us.

He had everything he had hoped to have
by that age — a well-paying job, a new house, a fancy car,
true love — but he still couldn't shake his jitters.

What the hell do you know about layout, anyhow?

And so, on the afternoon of the actual day,
he swung by his doctor
and had several units of Botox
injected into the slight furrows in his brow.

It was past midnight when we realized
that the sunscreen we were wearing had sparkles.

Thirty may have felt old to him,
but there was no reason he had to look it.

STUART ROSS

Pursuing a kind of gentle weirdness, Stuart Ross' poetry bends the details of everyday life into the strange and estranging form of a literary balloon animal. The exploitation and insertion of mismatched detail is an important tactic here. Take "Poem": a list of varying food dishes punctuated by an out-of-place introjection ("Help! I'm being —") and the name of Morris Fishbein, which seem merely weird until we clue in that poor Mr. Fishbein is literally on the menu. Ross excels at this kind of concision, creating newly messy fields of misunderstanding out of pieces that don't fit together. Although soft surrealism has become perhaps the most mainstream of avant-garde forms, Ross consistently pushes the technique in a masterful way, layering funny, outrageous imagery to construct crushing, affecting poems.

Long a stalwart of the Toronto small press scene, Stuart Ross is the author of seven books of poetry, two short-story collections, a book of personal essays, and a novel. He is the editor of the micropress Proper Tales and runs his own imprint at Mansfield Press.

Outline for a Blockbuster.
Publishers, Contact Me Directly.

Intersections are for sleeping in.

By "sleeping in" we refer to location and not duration.

Beds should be nailed to ceilings.

Everything at its own speed.

Money is enough.

The baker is a bad breadwinner.

Bread is bad.

We fit three in the trunk and save money at the drive-in.

"Smile for the tornado!"

My City Is Full of History

Your tenor saxophone is not my toaster oven.
Your winning smile is not my tax return.
When I opened the door at 3 a.m.
to insistent knocking: a stalk of celery,
rocking gently in the breeze.

You see, my city is full of history.
Goes back to before
I was born, or even you.
Mother put me on a toboggan
and gave a little nudge. She
never saw me again. Though
I saw her, every day,
walking by the store window
where I was a mannequin.

At the party:
imitation cheese product,
plus raisins, nestled into
the celery's long curl.
Through the window:
my aunt climbing up a tree.

I have avoided product placement
but play an acceptable
"Shadow of Your Smile"
on my toaster oven.

Poem

1. Pork spring roll with vermicelli.
2. Assorted flavours wheat gluten.
3. Tamarind chutney with samosa.
4. Help! I'm being —
5. Lentil and potato soup.
6. Mixed vegetable korma with cashews.
7. Mango and seasonal greens salad.
8. Tripe plus three kinds of mushroom.
9. Baked salmon teriyaki.
10. House-style penne arrabiata.
11. Morris Fishbein, chartered accountant.
12. Apple crumble with choice of ice cream.

JORDAN SCOTT

In these poems from his collection *Blert*, Jordan Scott runs us through a litany of words made material in an attempt not to represent his stutter but rather to investigate what a poetics emerging from his physical disability might sound like. On the page, the poems are filled with sharp and funny word combinations ("Gucci groin"; "Tupperware slur") coming directly out of words Scott has difficulty with — words that literally halt his speech.

In performance, we are confronted with Scott's difficulty with the words (the book is designed to be as difficult as possible for him to read aloud). As audience members, we become caught between the strange and funny combinations and the physical reality of Scott's stutter. In effect, we are dared to laugh by the material at the same time we are made uncomfortable by the reality of what we're laughing at, triggered by a social understanding that you're not supposed to laugh at the kid with the stutter.

Living in Vancouver, Jordan Scott is the author of *Silt* (New Star, 2005), *Blert* (Coach House Books, 2008), and *Decomp*, written in collaboration with Stephen Collis (Coach House Books, 2013). *Blert* was adapted into a short film for the Bravo network and was the subject of an online interactive documentary commissioned by the National Film Board of Canada.

Two Cheeseburgers, French Fries and a Coke

Twa, twaddle, Tweedledee, twas, twayblade, Tweedlededum, twat, tweezers, twinkle-toed, twig, twelve gauge, twin-engined, Twix, twizzle … zizz, zag, Zohar, zone, Zola, zoo, zonked, zoot suit, two

oo, o-o, oolong, oof, ooh, oodles, oom, oort, oozy … oops-a-daisy … een, eerie, eelworm, eek, eejit, eelgrass, eel, eelpout, eensy … chee, chee-chee, cheekbone, cheek, cheerful, cheeky … ye, yearly, yeasty, cheese

sea cow, sea lily, seamy seamstress, sea lion, sea lettuce, sea potato, sea moth, sea holly, sea gooseberry, sea dog, sea nettle, sea elephant, sea bee … beer, beetle, the bee's knees, beef … ff, FBI, ff, FBA, FB … bur, beef, bur, Burberry, burb, burgers

SSB, SSC, SSE, SSP, SSR, SST, SSW … WWF … fury, furuncle, fur seal … lee, leer, leek, leech … Chabrol, cha-cha … faff, French bean, French Congo, French bread, French cricket, French curve, French dressing, French

hiccup, hibachi, hickey, hide and seek, hi-fi … Fri, friendly fire, Freedom Fire, fries

SS, SSAFA … A, a, aargh, aardwolf, Ann Landers, Anna Banana, and

D, d, DA … A535, AAA, a

A, Aalborg, aardvark … kaka-beak, kaka-pants, kaka … AK, Akbar, akimbo … Co. c/o cocoa cabana, cockspur, cockeye bob, coconut palm, cock-up, cocksucker, cock and bull, cock block, cockatoo, cock-of-the-walk, cockpit, cochlea, cock-a-leekie, cock-eyed, Coca-Co, O … oak, oaktag, oakum, OAPEC … KKK, Kokanee, Koko, Kit Kat, Coke.

chomp set

    blubber tongue

*

if you must have an idea, have a short-term idea:

a Cocoa Puff
a two-step bluff
a fleeting rime

*

Broca's
camel clutch
grapple thalamus flux
box tonsils fresh black box
tongue scatter suckle polygon
syllable collar pop
mullet split end
leg lock glottal
lip off:

fresh nugs
mouse milking
NASCAR

wrist flex
snorkel mosh
dental furrow
Jell-O shot
ease Pantene

*

Coca-Cola tonic krill
gill baleen
dream wrenched
Kleenex smack
Baltic Pyrex
megahertz humpback
kickback: flex
nukes flub
blubber sexy
plankton number

*

Foreman rill
grill lisp
dental Whopper

Worcestershire

scaffold larynx
magma seethe
tarp gruff volcanic
ply canine

cusp
munch
crunch
rump

*

gales lurk
berserk cortex
honeyed botox
globs boom of clavicles
cornsilk lips blitz as
Molotov blisters
Tupperware slur

celeb Tex-Mex
thunder thigh

aerobic gulag
squeeze bottle
Gucci groin

*

bent tendon
each papyrus
fold cackles
buzz beatbox:
Kyzyl Kum Kyzyl Kum
shizzle cadence
cavum kinetic

COLIN SMITH

Composed of hypothetical questions and answers, Colin Smith's "Spot Quiz" exposes both idiotic logics and gaps in intelligence as we're asked to fill in the blanks on the other side of each of his one-liners. How are we expected to answer such unreasonable questions as "Whose ghost story are you?" What kind of question provokes the answer "Kafka's *Microwave Gourmet*"?

Smith's absurd disconnections create a space where we can puzzle over and laugh at the ways that knowledge is not entirely measureable (or, in the lingo of the classroom, *assessable*), or, in other words, the way educational institutions can never account for or fully control the sheer *weirdness* embedded in their structures. Smith recognizes the strangeness in the everyday organization of the classroom and challenges it by defamiliarizing the totally serious instrumental tool of the pop quiz, revealing its strangeness by making it strange.

Living in Winnipeg, Colin Smith is the author of *Multiple Poses* (Tsunami, 1997), *8x8x7* (Krupskaya, 2008), and *Carbonated Bippies!* (Nomados, 2012). He is a former member of the Kootenay School of Writing.

Spot Quiz

If a hen and a half lays an egg and a half in a day and a half, how long will it take Farmer Brown to plough his field using his left hand?

Having adopted Kevin's singular cough, Bonni's sardonic titter, and Suzanne's sidelong ironic glance, who am I?

Shove — Smash — Shoot — Burn — Run — Drive — Roam

Name the only jazz artist who has not recorded a version of Billy Strayhorn's "Lush Life."

John Hotdogs.

If Glenn Gould's food habits had been as varied as his drug intake ...

Reality, check one.

Are you a "without papers"?

True or False: Dentures give a true or false portrait of your face.

Yes, the door is part of the show.

Yes, the song is advocating ecological terrorism.

The differences between a novella.

Postulate a movie starring Kevin Costner, William Hurt, and Harrison Ford: Who's still awake after the first reel?

Lee M. Cardholder.

In the dictionary between *egg* and *emphysema*.

(a) It takes two feminists to change a light bulb: one to replace the bulb, the other to suck my cock; (b) God made men because dildos can't push lawnmowers.

Anything That Doesn't Move (a magazine for the adventurous necrophiliac).

Kafka's *Microwave Gourmet*.

A Dinner to Die For by Susan Dunlap and Pope John Paul I.

Give the last year in which it was possible for Luciano Pavarotti to see his own genitals without the aid of a reflective device.

If Clint Eastwood walked faster, shorter running times.

If you dream of having financial worries, does it mean that you are having tooth trouble?

Whose ghost story are you?

L7 — The Offspring — Sonic Youth — Nine Inch Nails — New Order — R.E.M. — The B-52's

Reality. Cheque bounces.

The Buzzcocks' influence on The Beatles.

The Mountie who slid off his whistle and blew his horse.

Did you have the ultimate coffee experience?

The GREAT DAY prosthesis is the answer to all your problems.

'Netizens are worth more than citizens.

Because.

110%.

Democracy™.

JONATHON WILCKE

These first five pages of Jonathon Wilcke's long poem "Dupe!" give us a glimpse into the comic circulations of Wilcke's text. Over the course of thirty-seven pages, he employs a kind of recycling as he returns to and rearticulates phrases in a way that adopts both the comic refrain of the callback and the musical refrain of blues. The *refrain* seems an important concept here, as it allows us to consider not only the way comedy can repeat but also how it can mutate — how it can "repeat to differ," to borrow a phrase from Brian Massumi. As Wilcke comes back to the thought of how the world is made gets him down (makes him blue), he dodges it in a different way, mining humour from our minor responses to the major impasses of life under late capitalism. [Also funny is the fact that "Jonathon" cannot spell his own name correctly. — Jonathan]

Jonathon Wilcke lives in Calgary and is the author of *Pornograph* (Red Deer, 2003) and *Dupe!* (Line, 2010). He is also a saxophonist, clarinetist, and composer who has performed both solo and with various groups throughout Western Canada. His first solo saxophone recording, *all erroRs Included*, and a clarinet recording, *Torn from the Akashic Record: Interactions with Acoustic Situations*, were released by UnCanadian Activities in 2013.

[from] Dupe!

floating somewhere
right above the virus of original thought
5 plus 7 no longer equals 12
feet hold socks up

sometimes the thought of how my world is made
    gets me down   makes me blue
sometimes i wonder if there's anything to do
but to up-quit this livin'
pre-board that plane
write an article or two   upright the tray
admit the trap   and the but
      enter the encyclopedia   visit
  the museum of foreign arts   clothe myself
   in a scruffy pink party dress and black army boots
    and later
      in black cutoff tights and black T-shirt
      with an inspired sheen of red

i spent all the money i won after suing McDonald's
for morbid obesity.

personally not withstanding obligation for hire:
lexicon of the licked.
a consummation alarm sirens
as the bride is confused by the broom
nothing is amiss   teens loitering at the 7-11
or hanging out   at the convenience store
        could this have been me:
elusive young stem cell unimpeachable potential
svelte disheveled suit me up to a mackerel supper all laid-up
on a bed of grains
tossed side-arm, unduly, improvidently into a barley field

drinking maple syrup under the northern lights, yup
drinking maple syrup under the aurora borealis, yup

it
doesn't take much to turn a sunny summer day
and the logic of a hole
into a tragedy:

last July at a Worcester pond,
 at a Dorchester street reservoir
 somebody dropped a teaspoon on the beach
 and a toddler drowned
  said a lifeguard at a lakefront birthday party
  in Claresholm

  she spits directly into the drain
  and watches the aqua foam
  wind down the pipe
  and starts to wash her hair
   she thinks about
   how people can drown
   in a teaspoon of water;
  it reminds her that no matter how familiar the routine
  she is never really safe

 and so she plugs all the sinks and shuts off the pipes

   but no one told her
   about the chocolate milk

last week
as Pastor Bill reminded the spectators
at the Aquatic Centre Baptism:
    god doesn't allow us to say
    "well, i've lived a good life"

    just

"i wish i wasn't born with a silver spoon in my mouth
or at least it could have been a slotted spoon"
when science, ethics, and morals clash
    in a waterspot   sometimes
    the thought of how my world is made
gets me down   makes me blue
sometimes i wonder   if there's anything to do
    but to up-quit this livin'   pre-board that plane
        use a spoon to scratch out my name
            just before i drown

and realize that i too am just a battery
hooked up: a man named maurice
led me down to middle earth

In these three poems from *Personals*, Ian Williams uses repetition, word replacement, and narrative to produce comic sparks in a lyric field. Like Elizabeth Bachinsky's poems, Williams' work combines a lyric expressiveness with a gentle experimentalism.

In "Dip," he adopts what looks like a banal pose ("Why didn't my friends show up?") that is undercut via a combination of mock-seriousness and light social network speak ("The friends I friended do not show"). In "Hay," he replaces most of the nouns in a chunk of text with "needle," producing an excessiveness that makes hay of the cliché. "Missed connections" plays with the form of the personal ad while suggesting a strange, surreal, incredible scene: With the ending line, Williams turns the poem suddenly, undercutting all of its lightheartedness to crushingly emphasize the actual *reason* why these people *must* connect, the desperation suddenly less funny now that it speaks to some shared trauma.

Living in Brampton, Ontario, Ian Williams is a poet and fiction writer. His books include the poetry collections *You Know Who You Are* (Wolsak and Wynn, 2010) and *Personals* (Freehand, 2012) as well as the short story collection *Not Anyone's Anything* (Freehand, 2011). He works as a professor at Sheridan College.

Dip

The friends I friended do not show.
One by one, yellow leaves, they text
— the snow, the snow, the snow, the snow —
sad emoticons of their faces.

One by one, down an arpeggio, they text
See you Monday. I will face them and
as always ☺ and ☺ and ☺ my face.
I'll say, Forget about it. I understand

On Monday I will have to face them and
the snow, the snow, the snow, the snow.
I'll say, Forget it. Really. I understand
the friends I friended did not show.

Hay

He was a young inner city needle who played
ball in a cage : what the needle were we thinking :
I would needle my hands in the chain-link needle
and needle him : he played with his needle
and his abs were needled like a half-eaten
Hershey needle :

                                        I had a
needle when I was seventeen : I told my needle I was
needle and he paid : we had needled each other : of course
it's needlable whether our needle was really a needle
when we decided to needle it : if it was a needle
I would name it Needle : we weren't allowed to needle
after the needle so we never talked about the needle :
my needle dropped out of needle and needled
a six-week certification needle : I needle saw him much :
needle once or twice he came back and brought me needles
for lunch and we needled our needles in the caf in silence
with our chopsticks : I needle you, he said :
I needle you too.

Missed connections: Walmart automotive dept — w4m — (Lunenburg MA)

You. At the Tire and Lube Express. You said *lube*
and I — did you notice? — revved. Your name tag
was missing so I read your hair, curled like a string of e's,
your forearms drizzled with soft hairs like a boy's
first moustache. Apart from that, you were built
like a walrus. The kind of man that drives a Ford
pickup. Black or silver. You said, *There might be a gas leak*
and *We can't fix that here, but don't worry, we'll get you fixed.*
By *fixed* you meant *hooked up*, by *hooked up* you meant
in touch with and meant nothing beyond *touch*.

Me. Volvo. Smelled like gasoline: I overfilled the tank
before the oil change. I took the package that comes
with a filter replacement. Have you already forgotten me?
I had trouble with the debit machine. Remember? You said,
Turn your card the other way — remember? — and took my hand,
not the card, took my hand with the card in it
and swiped it through. Remember. Please.
The gasoline. The woman almost on fire.

Part of a longer sequence, Daniel Zomparelli's "How to Get Washboard Abs — Fast!" interrogates the intersection of gay male culture and larger mainstream consumerism by laying out a series of one-liners that poke fun at the specific version of the subculture that has bled into the mainstream, from reality shows to sitcoms ("I'm sorry Ma'am your / Husband / has been / queer / eyed"). Zomparelli's jokey lines drift from cliché to critique and back again, unsettled and sometimes unsettling. "Meet me at the corner of commerce and gay culture," he suggests, nonchalantly opining that "you get the best gyros here." These lines seem tossed aside, but they are aimed square into the lap of straight, liberal North America — the part that has a gay best friend (which makes it *totally* not homophobic).

Daniel Zomparelli lives in Vancouver and is the author of *Davie Street Translations* (Talonbooks, 2012). He is the editor of *Poetry Is Dead* magazine and has written for or worked with a number of other magazines in Vancouver, including *Megaphone*, *Geist*, *Sad Mag*, and *Adbusters*.

How to Get Washboard Abs — Fast!

"I'm not gay, I'm from the future."
    — Christopher Nealon, *Plummet*

"Homos shoot photos of footlong schlongs."
    — Christian Bök, *Eunoia*

/// You keep saying / you're from the future,
but your BMW is a '95. // Used to
fuck in bathroom stalls,
and now you do / it in your
600-square-foot condo
before 9 p.m. because / the strata has been
concerned about
noise levels / and heteronormatizing. // The token
gay guy on
Big Brother
never wins.[1] // I'm sorry, Ma'am, your
husband
has been / queer- / eyed. // Have I
met you before, / Dumbledore?
// Did you / get a float in the / parade?
No, I'll just go
on the one for
Starbucks. It's half and half.

---

[1] In the American *Big Brother* of 2013, the gay guy finally won.

/// The guy
who designed
cutoff shirts
has all of
our money, let's
get him. //
Ricky Martin,
Clay Aiken,
and
Lance Bass
walk into
a bar. / I've gone too far, we forgot
about John Travolta / Me, I'm in love with my trainer. /
Neil Patrick Harris.
// The gay guy
on *Lost* had one
episode before
he blew up.

/// The economy
will be saved with same-sex-
themed wedding
cakes. // Don't ask,
don't tell,
don't miss out
on this offer, and
for the next three
minutes we'll throw
in a second Slap Chop
for free. // Have you planned

your gaycation yet? / Don't forget to use your
gay Air Miles. // Wait, wait,
wait, are you
a Jack gay or
a Will gay? // Meet me at
the corner
of commerce and
gay culture, you
get the best
gyros there. // Dildos can't
hug you
at night, but
they fill the void. // Capitalism is the
reproduction
of a butt-hole
in the shape of a flashlight.

/// Fact: 73% of American homes
have been designed
by two gay men
on a reality show. // Fact: I no longer
have to look
for gay subtext because
two seasons
into the new *90210*
they added their token gay guy. Fact: We don't talk about
Glee anymore. // P-C
isn't for M-E. // I bought
the Barcelona chair. Ate beef Wellington and cried bear
tears. Woof.

/// I buy *Butt Magazine* for
the articles. Living in a Gipsters paradise // American
Apparel
supports gay marriage and all I got was this lousy shirt. //
Bears and boners
over bedding. // Don't quit your
gay job, you will need
that when the gay
depression hits and
you are left without
a gay penny to
your gay name. // You might be an overweight / middle-
aged wife / who gets no respect, / has lost all confidence,
/ can't get a job, lost / a son, and can't afford / clothes, but
RuPaul / will help you at 8 p.m. / Pacific Standard Time.

/// Jock-strapped
to my work. // We tried to use K-Y Him and Her,
but we didn't know who should
use what. // I don't get it.
// I bought this because I wanted to have washboard abs,
and the guy in the magazine has washboard abs. // I
think he's hot because he looks like
he would beat me up, and I'm really
into guys who look like they'll beat
me up. // What about
the gay's gaze? // Rock Hudson / and a pack of smokes.
// Ginch by Gonch I Calvin Kleined
my way to the top. // Alt + Ctrl + Delete // Me

// Drag and drop
it into the folder. // Undo drag // I've been
using the
crystal method. // Unfrienemy // Don't worry, I'll just
retweet it.
// I'm such a stupid bitch,
I'm a stupid bitch. // Madonna
is sorry.
/// You put the homo
in home owner. / He had moulds
done of his cock, ass,
and mouth. I really
respect his
entrepreneurial nature. / DIY // Poke. / You don't
make friends with salad.
// Do you think he's sexier than me? // Carb break! //
I BBM you, you
BBM me, we BBM / each other.
// Hunting boots
from Brooklyn & Co., fishing
pants from Holt Renfrew,
plaid shirts from Armani,
beard from time.

/// What happens when several men
who work out all the time move
onto a magical island where
there is a shortage of T-shirts?
Find out next week on OUTtv. // Viewer discretion is
advised,

as there is generally no plot
to this TV show. // Gay vampires
is a little too symbolic. // The token British lady
is talking to the token gay guy
about the token black girl
on *House Wives of Washington DC*.
// The greatest gay
love story was
on a series about prisoners. // No one believes you, Vin
Diesel. // He looks sleepy,
does he bump?

/// I have a blog.
I have a gay blog.
I have an activist-oriented gay blog.
I have a porn-activist-orientated gay art blog.
I have a Tumblr account.
Butt: unplugged. //
God hates
a lot of things.
// Gay guys don't use edible chocolate
for romantic massages. // I was never very fierce,
Tyra fucking Banks. // No one is ever gay in a Disney film,
except maybe the fussy clock
in *Beauty and the Beast*. // Brian's cousin, Stan's
next-door neighbours, Big
Gay Al, Mr. Slave, Mr. Garrison,
Chandler's dad,
but not Lenny and Carl,
not yet.

// The Twink-ee Defence.

/// Perpetually jaded,
I hate being from the future. / Fuck you, society,
said the tattoo. / You don't even
know me. / If you're looking for me, I'll be under the rain-
bow balloon arch during the pride parade in the Speedos
and air-brushed corporate logo tattoos. / Mazda Miata my
medulla oblongata / He overdosed /
on liberation.

Acknowledgements

We would like to thank the authors for agreeing to be in a book called *Why Poetry Sucks*, and their publishers for agreeing to allow them to agree.

Ryan would like to thank Haida Arsenault-Antolick, Michael Barnholden, Stephen Collis, Amy De'Ath, Jeff Derksen, Janey Dodd, Chris Ewart, Joseph Giardini, Scott Inniss, Natalie Knight, Danielle LaFrance, Andrew McEwan, Patrick Morrison, Alex Muir, Cecily Nicholson, and Sean O'Brien for their thoughtful, useful, and funny conversations about jokes, poems, and anthologies. Extra-special thanks to Kim O'Donnell for her keen edits and incisive critiques of this book's introduction.

Jonathan would like to thank rappers, coffee, and Jon Paul Fiorentino for making this book possible. Thanks also to Dan Varrette, Mike O'Connor, and everyone at Insomniac Press for making it really possible. Thanks, as always, to Mandy Heyens and Jessie Taylor for everything they do that they don't even realize makes things possible.

Ryan and Jonathan were going to thank each other but ultimately decided that it wouldn't allow them to complain about how anthology editing is thankless work. So, fuck Ryan. And fuck Jonathan too. Seriously.

More Acknowledge-y Acknowledgements

"Cuntajunta" and "Squaw Guide" by Annharte. From *Indigena Awry*, copyright © 2012 Marie Baker [Annharte]. Reprinted with the permission of the author and New Star Books.

"Prank!" by Oana Avasilichioaei and Erín Moure. From *Expeditions of a Chimæra*, copyright © 2009 Oana Avasilichioaei and Erín Moure. Reprinted with the permission of the authors and BookThug.

"Nails" and "I Want to Have a Chuck and Di Party Like My Parents Did in the '80s" by Elizabeth Bachinsky. From *The Hottest Summer in Recorded History*, copyright © 2013 Elizabeth Bachinsky. Reprinted with the permission of the author and Nightwood Editions. "[from] Lead the Wants" by Elizabeth Bachinsky. From *CURIO: Grotesques and Satires from the Electronic Age*, copyright © 2005, 2009 Elizabeth Bachinsky. Reprinted with the permission of the author and BookThug.

"Psalm," "Comedy," and "Relieving" by Gary Barwin. From *The Porcupinity of the Stars*, copyright © 2010 Gary Barwin. Reprinted with the permission of the author and Coach House Books.

"January 28, 1986" by derek beaulieu. Reprinted with the permission of the author. "Nothing Odd Can Last" by derek beaulieu. From *How to Write*, copyright © 2010

About the Editors

Ryan Fitzpatrick is a poet and critic living in Vancouver, where he is pursuing a doctorate at Simon Fraser University with work on the relationship between contemporary poetics and the social production of space. He is the author of *Fake Math* (Snare, 2007) and *Fortified Castles* (Talonbooks, 2014).

Jonathan Ball, Ph.D. (English), teaches literature, film, and writing at the University of Manitoba and the University of Winnipeg. He is the author of the poetry books *Ex Machina* (BookThug, 2009), *Clockfire* (Coach House Books, 2010), and *The Politics of Knives* (Coach House Books, 2012; winner of a Manitoba Book Award) and the academic monograph *John Paizs's "Crime Wave"* (U of Toronto P, 2014). Visit him at JonathanBall.com.

Ryan and Jonathan previously collaborated on a special issue of the poetics journal *Open Letter* titled "Why Are You Laughing?" where they examined the relationship between contemporary experimental poetics and humour.